Defensive Handgun
for the
Armed Citizen

Eddie B. Hulsey

First published by AuthorHouse 3/2/2009

ISBN: 978-1-4389-4892-8

Printed in the United States of America
Bloomington, Indiana

Dedication

My job often takes me away from my family, but they always seem to understand. To my wife, of more than 20 years, Jacqueline thank you for your love, understanding, friendship, and everything you do for me and our family. I've very much enjoyed the ride, and look forward to growing old with you.

To my children – Chad, Chris and Catie, I love and cherish each of you. Life would be so dull without you all!

Chad, sometimes I believe I've learned as much from you as you have from me. Being the first, you did not come with an instruction manual, but you have turned out to be a great person. Keep your adventurous, fun loving spirit – it will serve you well in life.

Chris, you are so competitive and such a neat young man. Keep striving for your dreams and they will come true.

Catie, you are a princess in my eye. No doubt you were a gift from God. Continue to be the sweet girl you are.

To my parents, Boyd and Dessie, who set me on the right road early in life, which helped make me what I am today.

This book is dedicated to my loving family. They, like the loved ones of everyone reading this book, are why we need to prepare ourselves for our own self defense and that of our loved ones!

Table of Contents

Forward

While it is true that crime rates have been falling in recent years, the fact remains that violent and property crime continue to be concerns to average Americans. Reviewing crime statistics for the last 20 years reveals there have been almost 32 million Americans victimized by violent criminals. Add to that the 225 million property crimes committed, and one sees that almost 258 million Americans have been victimized in the last 20 years. Given the 2007 United States population, a full 85% of Americans have fallen prey to the criminal element.

No wonder that the number of concealed weapon permits is on the rise in this country. Fortunately, states have seen the wisdom in passing concealed carry statutes so the average citizen can legally carry handguns for their self protection – and citizens have been taking advantage of this right.

This book is written for the armed citizens of the United States. However, there is plenty of information that will be useful to the law enforcement reader. I have organized the book so that the first chapter addresses the need for personal self defense. In this chapter, I explore the national crime rates and the fact that law enforcement does not have an obligation to protect each individual citizen.

Chapter 2 deals with what justifies the use of deadly force. Concepts on self defense are explored in this chapter as well. Various court cases are discussed that deal with the right to self defense, as are identification of state self defense laws.

Analysis results of deadly force confrontations are presented in Chapter 3. This information provides the self defense handgunner with what a lethal force confrontation most likely will be like. This information should be very useful to law enforcement officers, as well as the armed citizen, because the statistics provided come from officer involved shootings.

Defensive handgun selection is covered in Chapter 4. Various weapon types and actions are discussed. Selecting handgun ammunition that will be most effective is also covered in this chapter. Scientific studies for determining the most effective caliber and ammunition are presented in this chapter to support my recommendations.

No one can be too safe with firearms. Chapter 5 is devoted to firearms safety. Safety aspects for carrying and storing firearms are covered. There is a section on guns and children and how to inoculate young children from firearm accidents. This chapter is highly important to all.

Tactics and techniques for the defensive handgunner come in Chapter 6. Individual tactics and techniques are provided to ensure the survivability of the defensive handgunner. Defensive planning is discussed, with examples of home defense plans given. Inside and outside the home defense options are presented, with a section addressing vehicle defense situations as well.

Most combat instructors, both military and civilian, agree that the mind is the most deadly weapon one carries into combat. Without proper development and deployment of this most important weapon, luck becomes the only factor in survivability. Chapter 7 provides details on how to mentally prepare for the battle ahead.

People do not become good at a skill without practice. Consider professional athletes and the time spent preparing for games. Many, many more hours are devoted to practice than it takes to complete a competitive athletic event. So should it be for the defensive handgunner. In Chapter 8 I discuss practice ammunition, targets, and practice routines. Also presented are a number of realistic courses of fire that can help the defensive handgunner be successful in a self defense situation.

One can easily train ones self for the physical skills needed to emerge victorious from a self defense incident. They, too, can prepare themselves mentally so that the most powerful weapon is equally employed properly during such incidents. However, few give thought to the after effects of a self defense use of deadly force. Not only will there be personal effects from this, but most likely there will be legal effects. It would be a shame to survive a deadly force encounter, only to be wrongly arrested, tried and convicted for a legal defense of oneself or another. Therefore, Chapter 9 is devoted to help prepare you to survive the legal aspects of a justifiable use of deadly force, as well as to point out mental issues that may have a devastating effect if they are not properly dealt with.

Chapter 10 provides information on the various state laws governing concealed carry. This chapter is useful in helping you understand what the concealed carry laws are for your state. Furthermore, it covers transporting your weapon to other states, with a section on flying armed and what the rules are for doing so.

Finally, Chapter 11 provides information on where to obtain additional information on defensive handgunning.

I want to thank you for buying my book. It is my sincere hope that you obtain useful information in your pursuit of being an armed citizen. Thank you!

Chapter 1

The Personal Need for Self Defense

The police cannot protect the citizen at this stage of our development, and they cannot even protect themselves in many cases. It is up to the private citizen to protect himself and his family, and this is not only acceptable, but mandatory.

Jeff Cooper

Jeff Cooper's quote is chilling in the bare, unblemished fact that the police cannot protect its citizens from violent crime. For those of you who did not know Jeff Cooper, he is better known as the father of modern pistol technique. In 1976 Colonel Cooper founded what is now known as Gunsite Training Center and began teaching defensive pistol techniques. He served in the Marine Corp during both World War II and the Korean War, where he learned his gunfighting skills first hand. What he learned during those wars was shared with law enforcement and civilian students interested in defensive firearms. This quote is even more remarkable when you consider the fact that courts have actually ruled that police are not obligated to protect the citizenry they are sworn to "protect and serve."

In the 1981 case of *Warren vs. District of Columbia* the D.C. Court of Appeals ruled that police are not liable for failure to provide adequate police protection. This case was based on the fact that two men broke into a home shared by three women in the Northwest section of the District of Columbia. Two women shared space in an upper floor, while the third woman shared space with her young child on the lower floor.

The two suspects in this case sexually assaulted the

woman on the lower floor of the house. Screams were heard by the woman's two roommates, and they promptly called the police for help. The DC dispatcher did indeed dispatch cars to the residence, but gave it a low priority for response.

An officer drove through the alley behind the residence and around to the front, but did not stop. Another officer knocked on the residence's door, but after getting no answer, left. This was all observed by the victim's roommates, who had crawled out onto the roof.

After the police left, the victim's roommates reentered the house. Still hearing screams, they called police a second time and told them their roommate was still being assaulted. The police dispatcher once again dispatched officers, but dispatched it as "investigate the trouble" – a very low priority.

After the victim stopped screaming, her roommates called down to the victim. Unbeknownst to them, the two assailants were still in the home. Knowing additional victims were present, the assailants forced the first victim upstairs with her two roommates. For the next fourteen hours the two assailants sexually assaulted the three women.

Fortunately for these three victims the suspects chose not to kill them. The victims filed a law suit against the city, which was dismissed based on the fundamental principle that a government and its agents are under no general duty to provide public service, such as police protection, to an individual – this general duty applies only to the public at large. Therefore, the trial court dismissed the suit. Subsequently, the DC Court of Appeals upheld this dismissal based on the "general duty" not being specific to individuals – only to the "public at large."

If the fact that police are under no "general duty" to protect the individual citizen does not clearly define the need for developing defensive handgun skills for self protection, then maybe the facts revealed in the Federal Bureau of Investigation (FBI) Uniform Crime Report (UCR) will underscore this need.

In 1929 the International Association of Chiefs of Police (IACP) determined there was a need for a national crime reporting system, which resulted in today's UCR. However, it was not until 1930 that the FBI was tasked with collecting, analyzing, reporting and archiving these crime statistics.

2007 was the most recent report published by the FBI at the time of this writing. The results are startling. A total of 1,408,337 violent crimes were reported in 2007 throughout the United States. Violent crime, as defined by the FBI in the UCR, consists of murder and non-negligent manslaughter, forcible rape, robbery, and aggravated assault. The following table provides the number of each violent crime committed.

VIOLENT CRIME	OFFENSES
Murder	16,929
Forcible Rape	90,427
Robbery	445,125
Aggravated Assault	855,856
TOTAL	1,408,337

Table 1 – Violent Crime

These are just numbers to some people, but to me they represent much more. Sixteen thousand, nine hundred and twenty-nine people were killed by criminals; ninety thousand, four hundred and twenty-seven women were forcibly raped by scum; four hundred and forty-five thousand, one hundred and twenty five innocents had their property forcibly taken from them; and eight hundred and fifty-five thousand, eight hundred and fifty six people were assaulted in an aggravated manner. All of this in what is supposed to be a civilized country. It is enough to make your blood boil, and should be the impetus for wanting to learn to use a handgun in self-defense.

Additionally, there were 9,843,481 property crimes reported this same year. According to the FBI definition, property crimes consist of burglary, theft-larceny, and motor vehicle theft.

The following table provides the number of each property crime.

PROPERTY CRIME	OFFENSES
Burglary	2,179,140
Theft-Larceny	6,568,572
Motor Vehicle Theft	1,095,769
TOTAL	9,843,481

Table 2 – Property Crime

Again, these represent more than just numbers to me – they represent innocent people who were victimized by the low lifes of our society. I will not belabor the point. Suffice it to say that more than nine million people (almost 10 million) were victims of property crimes. Combining violent and property crime numbers, more than 11 million of our fellow citizens were preyed on by the dregs of society during 2007. The police cannot be everywhere all the time, so these innocent victims were unprotected and vulnerable.

And the very sad part of all of these statistics is that it actually represents a year in which the crime rate was down.

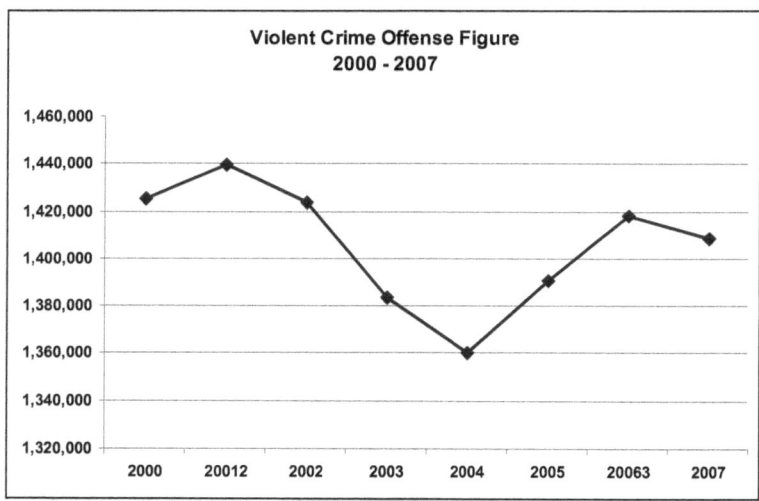

Figure 1 – Violent Crime Offenses

4

The crime trend from 2000 through 2007 is shown in Figure 1.

What does all of this mean to you as a citizen? It means that 466 out of every 100,000 citizens were victims of violent crime, and 3,263 of every 100,000 citizens were victims of property crime. Therefore, each of us has a 3,729 chance in 100,000 of being a victim of either a reported violent or property crime.

There are studies that suggest many crimes, such as rape, are not reported to police. This means the odds of being a victim are actually higher than that reported in the FBI UCR. And of course, these numbers do not take into account the citizens who were armed and defended themselves – thus not becoming a crime statistic.

Gary Kleck and Marc Gertz conducted a study on how many people in the United States had actually used a gun in self-defense. The results of the study were published in 1995 in the Northwestern University School of Law, Journal of Criminal Law and Criminology, and was entitled, "Armed Resistance to Crime: The Prevalence and Nature of Self Defense With A Gun." What their study revealed was that there were approximately 2,549,862 cases of armed citizens utilizing firearms to protect themselves in self defense each year. This is proof positive that we do not have to succumb to criminals by becoming victims.

These statistics, taken from authoritative sources, clearly reveal the prevalence of crime in the United States. They should be a glaring reason why we, as citizens, must prepare to protect ourselves, our loved ones, and our possessions – for if the police cannot protect us, we must do so ourselves.

Fortunately, 40 states have recognized the need for citizen self-defense and codified their right to carry firearms for self-defense. More on these states is provided in later chapters.

Chapter 2

Deadly Force

and

Concepts of Self Defense

We continue to be exasperated by the view, apparently gaining momentum in certain circles, that armed robbery is okay as long as nobody gets hurt! The proper solution to armed robbery is a dead robber, on the scene.
Jeff Cooper

Some may think that Colonel Cooper's quote is callus, but when in fear of your life the ability to use deadly force is very reassuring. There are hundreds of definitions of deadly force, but the general substance in all are the same. Deadly force is nothing more than that amount of force that is reasonable to believe will cause death or serious bodily injury to the recipient.

Defining deadly force is easy. Understanding when it can be legally used is somewhat more complex. The primary reason for the complexity of understanding the legal use of deadly force is that we live in a republic where each State is allowed to make its own laws. Consequently, the United States does not have one legal definition of deadly force, but rather has one in each of the fifty states and territories of this great nation. Knowing when you can legally use deadly force is the most important thing when it comes to defending yourself.

The concept of self defense has its beginning in Roman times, and was adopted in the United States as a result of

English Common Law. It has been codified by each of the states and territories of the United States. Each state has its own legal definitions for when deadly force can be used in self defense, but they all have in common the following three times deadly force is legal:

1. To defend oneself against imminent death or great bodily harm
2. To defend a third party against imminent death or great bodily harm
3. To prevent a forcible felony from being committed against oneself or a third party

There are a number of key words that need to be fully understood in this list of justifications for the use of deadly force.

First, what does imminent mean? Well, simply put it means immediate. Let's look at some examples of what may or may not be considered imminent.

You are outside your house doing lawn work when a particularly obnoxious neighbor comes into his yard across the street and begins to verbally abuse and threaten you. He is wearing shorts, flip flops and no shirt. He obviously is not armed with any type of weapon or object that can be used as a weapon. Are his verbal threats enough to believe you are in imminent danger of being killed or severely beaten? No, they are not.

Now change this scenario to where the neighbor has a baseball bat in his hands and tells you he will bash your head in. Do you believe you are in imminent danger? No, probably not because he is still across the street in his own yard without making any movements toward you. You can simply go into the house and call the police.

Same basic scenario, but now let's place a gun in the obnoxious neighbor's hand and he is beginning to raise the weapon and point it in your direction. Are you now in imminent danger? Yes, most likely you would feel that you are; therefore, you would be justified in defending yourself by means up to and including the use of deadly force.

Great bodily harm is the next term that needs to be understood. What is it? In a 2003 State Appeals Court (Washington State in the case of State of Washington, Respondent vs. Lester Dane Blanton II) ruling, great bodily harm was defined as "bodily injury that creates a probability of death, or which causes significant serious permanent disfigurement, or that causes a significant permanent loss or impairment of the function of any bodily part or organ."

Revisiting our earlier scenario, what if your neighbor was pointing a child's play pistol at you? Would your use of deadly force preclude the notion of self defense? The fact that the pistol was a toy was not known to you, so you would in fact have a fear of imminent death or great bodily harm.

Forcible felony is the next term in the list of justifiable reasons for using deadly force. What is a forcible felony? Recall the categories of violent crime – murder, forcible rape, robbery, and aggravated assault. These are all forcible felonies. Murder and forcible rape do not need further explanation, but what constitutes robbery and aggravated assault?

Robbery is the taking of money or property by force or the fear of physical injury. Robbery can take the form of purse snatching, carjacking, mugging, or a host of similar street slang offenses. The bottom line is that the theft was either by force or the threat of force. Consider you are walking to your car with your wife when someone approaches you from behind and presses something hard in your back and demands your wallet. This is robbery. This is a forcible felony. This justifies your use of deadly force to prevent the taking of your wallet. So what if the suspect is holding a cigarette lighter instead of a gun? The point is that the threat of force was being used to steal your wallet.

Aggravated assault is when someone attempts to cause serious bodily injury to another. No weapon necessarily has to be involved in such an assault. The simple fact of a

See https://

ferocious unarmed attack by a larger attacker can be considered aggravated assault, and justify the use of deadly force.

As a former police officer, I had several occasions to work incidents that involved self defense issues. One of the most tragic such incidents I worked occurred between two young males who were apparently seeing the same young lady. The spurned one of the two decided to try to intimidate the other by blocking his vehicle, getting out of his car, and pointing a black BB pistol at the other young man. However, the victim was not going to be intimidated. He reached into the back floorboard of his car, withdrew a 12 gauge shotgun, and fired it at the aggressor. The first shot hit the aggressor in the weapon hand. It demolished the cheap BB pistol and partially amputated the aggressor's trigger finger. The victim racked the slide of the shotgun, chambering another round, and fired a second time at the aggressor. The victim racked the shotgun again, chambered a round, and fired a third shot, which went into the back of the aggressor. There were no charges filed against the victim for this incident.

How and why were no charges brought you might ask? First, the aggressor blocked the victim's vehicle preventing his departure and brandished a black handgun, pointing it at the victim. It was dark, so the victim had no way of knowing that this was anything other than a real handgun. Therefore, the victim was justified in defending himself from imminent death or great bodily harm.

But he shot him in the back! How did he get away with that? Gunshot victims are often shot in the back, some are intentional and many are accidental. Think about it. If you are being shot at, or have already been hit, and have no way of protecting yourself, your first instinct may be to turn and run away. This is classic "fight or flight" syndrome that is a part of our gene pool from long ago.

Consider that it takes approximately six-tenths of a second for a human being to turn 180 degrees from the way they are facing. This is the same approximate time it takes to pull the trigger of a firearm. For that reason, it is entirely conceivable that the last trigger pull was occurring at the exact instant that the aggressor was turning to run away. In fact, in this case the aggressor was found collapsed behind a building that was about a quarter of a mile away.

Fortunately for the aggressor, the victim had his 12 gauge loaded with bird shot; otherwise, this altercation would have been fatal for the aggressor.

As one can see, complexities are present in using deadly force in self defense situations, even with it clearly evident and legal to use deadly force to defend oneself.

In determining justification for the use of deadly force, one can rely on the AOJ Triad for further guidance. The term AOJ Triad was coined by Massad Ayoob in a series of magazine articles in 1991, and is taught to law enforcement officers to help them in assessing the facts surrounding a shooting incident. The acronym AOJ stands for Ability, Opportunity and Jeopardy. Without all of these present, law enforcement officers are taught they are not justified in shooting someone. Let's explore each of these concepts.

AOJ Triad

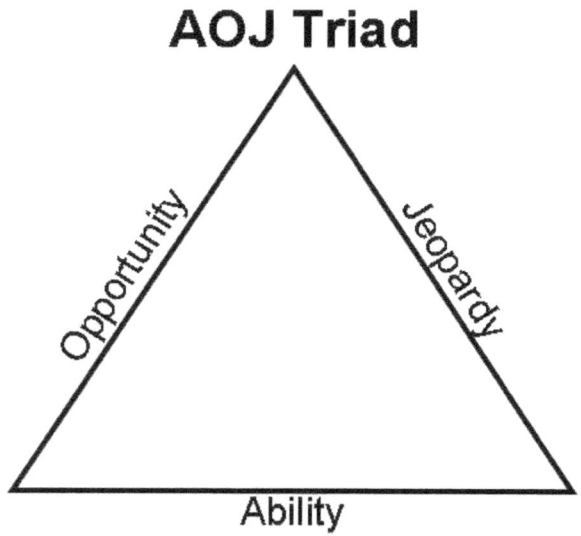

Figure 2 – AOJ Triad

Ability refers to whether the aggressor has the means to inflict death or great bodily harm to the victim. Ability does not simply refer to an aggressor having a firearm or other weapon such as a knife, but runs a broad gamut of definitions. A baseball bat, two-by-four, brick, rock, pipe, chain, ax, chainsaw, ice pick, machete, garrote, hammer, chair, broken bottle, pool stick, personal weapons (hands, fists, feet, etc.) and many other everyday items have been used as weapons to kill. These can certainly provide someone the ability to kill or cause great bodily harm.

Disparity of force is another concept that can be used in determining an aggressor's ability to cause death or great bodily harm. That is a male overwhelming a smaller female, or a larger male overwhelming a smaller male with nothing but their hands, feet, elbow, knees, head, etc to the point of causing death or great bodily harm. Another example of disparity of force is someone trained in pugilistic arts (i.e., amateur or professional boxer with training and special skills, the martial artist who is trained in using their body parts as weapons, and a military person who has a great deal of hand-to-hand training) attacking someone not so trained.

Opportunity refers to whether the aggressor is in a position to use their ability to cause death or great bodily harm. Recall our earlier scenario dealing with an obnoxious neighbor. In the first scenario he was simply verbally abusing, which has him without the ability or the opportunity. Then we placed a baseball bat in his hands, and then he had the ability (e.g., the baseball bat), but probably didn't have the opportunity because he was still located across the street and was not moving toward you. Finally in that series of scenarios, the obnoxious neighbor had a handgun. This provides him with both the ability and the opportunity to cause death or great bodily harm.

Jeopardy is the final side to the triad, and means that the aggressor is acting in such a manner that the defender, and a reasonable person, would conclude that the defender is in imminent danger of death or great bodily harm.

Previous court cases, involving the use of deadly force in self defense, make mention of the "reasonable person standard" in determining justification for the use of deadly force. What is the reasonable person standard? Simply put, it is what a fictional person (the reasonable person) who has an ordinary degree of reason, prudence, care, foresight, etc. would have concluded if put in the same position as that of the victim. Reasonableness is based on the totality of the circumstances surrounding an incident. If one cannot articulate the sequence of events in such a way as to allow this fictional reasonable person to place themselves in a position of the victim in a self defense incident and come to the same conclusion as the victim, then the shooting will not be ruled justified.

All three – Ability, Opportunity, and Jeopardy must be present in order for the use of deadly force in a self defense situation to be justifiable.

Another law enforcement concept taught to police is the force continuum. The force continuum provides various levels of force that should be progressively phased through before an officer uses deadly force, if circumstances allow. It is intended to train officers that varying levels of force, short of deadly force, are available for apprehending a suspect. Courts have held from the earliest case law on file, that force greater than that being used by a suspect is necessary in order for an officer to overcome a resisting offender.

Law enforcement has always used a progressive level of force. This progression is ultimately determined by the offender. That is, when an offender ceases resisting arrest then the officer will stop escalating the use of force.

I still remember what my father, who is a retired Shift Commander of the largest sheriff's department in Northeast Georgia, told me when I went into law enforcement. "You treat people the way they let you treat them." This is a different twist on the old adage that you treat people the way you want to be treated. This advice was given to me in 1979 when I was beginning my law enforcement career, which was 12 years after he had gone into law enforcement. By that time he had plenty of experience in treating people the way they would let him.

What he meant, and went on to say, was that if people would let you be nice to them – then be nice. If they wanted you to be rough with them, then be rougher than them and get the job done.

Of course this advice came from the man who told me when I was young and in school that if I ever started a fight he would give me a whipping, and if he ever found out that I ran from a fight he would give me a whipping. I never tested his word on this because I knew he meant what he said. His advice has served me well.

So what exactly is the force continuum? There are a number of models out there. Some have fewer phases, and others have more phases than I present here, but they all are very consistent in the increasing levels of force. The current force continuum is:

1. Presence
2. Verbal Commands
3. Empty Hand
   a. Soft Hand (Hands used to guide, hold, restrain)
   b. Hard Hand (Kicks, punches, other striking techniques)
4. Pepper spray, baton, Taser
5. Less Lethal (Bean bags, rubber bullets, netting, etc.)
6. Deadly Force

The lowest level of force is officer presence. Many hostile situations can be calmed and resolved simply by a uniformed officer appearing on the scene. However, if mere presence does not cease offender resistance, then the next step is verbal commands. An officer will tell offenders to stop what they are doing and to submit to arrest.

If presence and verbal commands do not end offender resistance, then an officer will escalate force to empty hand techniques. Some force continuums further break empty hand into two categories – soft hand and hard hand.

Soft hand force techniques consist of an officer using their hands to guide, hold, or restrain a suspect until handcuffs can be applied and the offender brought under arrest. The next phase would be hard hand techniques, which include punches, kicks, and other striking techniques, which are intended to subdue an offender until handcuffs can be applied and the offender brought under arrest.

Fourth in the order of progression is the use of force tools that include pepper spray, batons, Tasers®, flashlights, and other striking weapons. The striking weapons in this phase are high on the use of force spectrum because bludgeoning can and has caused death. Therefore, officers must be careful to strike non-fatal areas when employing this level of force.

A fairly new phase has been added, which is less-lethal. These are tools that have been developed that are meant to be short of deadly force, but may still utilize a weapon to deploy them. Examples include bean bag rounds, weapon deployed netting, and rubber bullets. There have been documented deaths caused by these so called less-lethal devices, but many agencies are using these in lieu of progressing to deadly force.

And finally on the force continuum is deadly force, which is administered via use of an officer's weapon.

Many defensive tactics instructors, both in the martial arts and firearms arena, are now subscribing to implementation of a force continuum for personal self defense by civilians. I vehemently disagree with this! Unlike law enforcement officers who deal with many types of people that they must arrest, civilians using their firearms in self defense need to think of only the front sight when faced with a deadly force situation. Civilians should not be concerned with force escalation when confronted by an armed robber or a crazed murderer. Quickly getting their weapon into their hand, acquiring the target, concentrating on the front sight, and pressing the trigger is what a civilian should focus on during a deadly force situation. Taking a quote from Lou Holtz, civilian's acting in self-defense must **WIN**, which means they must do **WHAT'S IMPORTANT NOW**!

A final concept needs addressing with regard to self defense and the use of deadly force, and that is a discussion on the "duty to retreat" and Castle Doctrine. With most laws in the United States, these two concepts have their original underpinnings in Old English Common law.

Duty to retreat comes from an old common law case that required noblemen to "retreat to the wall" when someone entered their castle before they were justified in the use of deadly force. Many states within the United States still have duty to retreat laws. However, another common law concept – the Castle Doctrine – comes into play. Whereas, the Castle Doctrine states that if you are in your own home (e.g., your Castle) you expect to be safe from attack. Therefore, one is justified in the use of deadly force to protect their Castle.

Due to the contradictions posed by these two concepts, many states have passed in recent years "stand your ground" or "stay and fight" statutes. Commonly, these statutes provide that if a person is in a location they have the right to be, then they are justified in the use of deadly force for self defense purposes.

There is federal case law to support the "stand your ground" concept. In the 1895 case of Beard vs. United States, the Supreme Court ruled that:

> *A man assailed on his own grounds, without provocation, by a person armed with a deadly weapon and apparently seeking his life is not obliged to retreat, but may stand his ground and defend himself with such means as are within his control….*

In a 1905 Minnesota case State vs. Gardner, the judge acquitted Gardner, who killed a man who was attempting to kill him with a rifle. The Judge in that case wrote:

> *The doctrine of "retreat to the wall" had its origin before the general introduction of guns. Justice demands that its application have due regard to the general use of and to the type of firearms. It would be good sense for the law to require, in many cases, an attempt to escape from a hand to hand encounter with fists, clubs, and even knives, as a justification for killing in self-defense; while it would be rank folly to require when experienced men, armed with repeating rifles, face each other in an open space, removed from shelter, with intent to kill or cause great bodily harm.*

As I previously stated, many states still have duty to retreat laws, but many more are now passing "stand your ground" and/or "Castle Doctrine" laws. The following are state listings of the various types of laws currently on the books:

States with Stand Your Ground Laws

There is no duty to retreat in the following states.

- Alabama
- Arizona
- Florida
- Georgia
- Indiana
- Kentucky
- Louisiana
- Oklahoma
- South Carolina
- Texas
- Tennessee
- Washington

States with Castle Doctrine Laws

Recall that Castle Doctrine Laws provide that there is no "duty to retreat" when in your home. Many of these state's Castle Laws apply to your vehicles as well.

- Alaska
- Colorado
- Connecticut
- Hawaii
- Maine
- Maryland
- Massachusetts
- Michigan
- Mississippi

- Missouri
- Ohio
- New Jersey
- North Carolina
- Rhode Island
- West Virginia
- Wyoming
- New Hampshire

States with Weak Castle Doctrine Laws

In the following states, the "duty to retreat" has not been removed; however, deadly force may be justified to end a home invasion where no imminent lethal threat is presented by the invader.

- Idaho
- Illinois
- Minnesota

- Montana
- New York
- Utah

States with No Castle Doctrine Laws

- Iowa
- Pennsylvania
- Virginia

In the listing of states that I found there are only 38 states that have clear enough statutes to determine their "duty to retreat," "Stand you Ground," and "Castle Doctrine" stance on these important concepts for self defense. Consequently, as an armed citizen understanding the need for self defense, you must take it upon yourself to research your particular state's law regarding these issues. Know what your rights are!

Chapter 3

Analyzing Confrontation

We sleep safe in our beds because rough men stand ready in the night to visit violence on those who would do us harm.

George Orwell

Unfortunately there is no federal agency tasked with tracking armed confrontations between offenders and citizens. Therefore, it is difficult to draw conclusions on what these types of confrontations most typically look like. However, the FBI is tasked with tracking such information on officer involved shootings. These findings are published annually in the *Law Enforcement Officers Killed and Assaulted* Report. I have been analyzing these reports for more than twenty years, and have found the data to be very enlightening with regards to important circumstances surrounding these tragic officer deaths.

Since there is little data available regarding civilian involved shooting incidents, what better place for the armed citizen to turn for information that can be used in their future survival than that provided by the proud and brave law enforcement officers who have made the ultimate sacrifice so that you and I and our families can live in relative safety. As Orwell would agree, sleep safe in your beds because these men and women stand ready to do violence on your behalf, but realize they do not absolve you of your responsibility to defend yourself, your family and others when these officers are engaged elsewhere.

The data I am about to share with regard to armed confrontations is the result of an analysis I conducted of the last 10 years of officers killed and assaulted. Numbers of officers killed each year do fluctuate, just as the crime rate in America fluctuates. However, there is a relative constant in these numbers and the underlying facts surrounding the circumstances involved at the time of an officer's death. Hence, these are useful representations of what an armed confrontation will look like, and should be taken to heart by the armed citizen contemplating their own self defense.

Characteristics of a Cop Killer

What does a typical cop killer look like? Is there a profile for the violent offender that kills a cop? There truly is no single profile of a cop killer that would allow someone simply to look at a person to determine if they are prone to violence, so all potential offenders must be treated equally. From the perspective of a civilian who is trying to protect themselves, every unknown person must be observed in a skeptical light until their intentions are known. The following profile of the typical cop killer can be used by the civilian in determining the amount of skepticism they should show to an unknown person in a location where self defense may be needed.

Based on ten years of statistical data, the average age of a cop killer is 29, with 70% ranging in age from 18 to 35 years of age. They are typically five feet, 10 inches tall and weigh 176 pounds. Fifty-six percent are white, 41% are black, and the remaining 3% are of other races. Ninety-eight percent of the perpetrators are male. Eighty percent have a criminal history, with 25% being under judicial supervision of some sort at the time of the confrontation. Twenty-three percent are known to the officer's agency. And 20% are determined to be under the influence of drugs or alcohol at the time of confrontation.

Time of Confrontation

If you are reading this book, then I suspect you are

contemplating your own self defense. You may already own a defensive handgun and practice with it regularly, you may own one and practice only periodically, or you do not own one but are thinking about getting one. Whatever your situation, you probably think going to the range during the day is the best, and may be accustomed to firing in daylight hours only. If this describes you or your perception of when the best time to practice your firearms skills are, be aware you may not be preparing for the correct encounter.

Fifty-six percent of all law enforcement officer deadly encounters occur during the hours of darkness. The following table breaks down the percentage of when fatal law enforcement shootings have occurred over 10 years.

Total A.M. hours	38%
12:01 a.m. - 2 a.m.	10%
2:01 a.m. - 4 a.m.	6%
4:01 a.m. - 6 a.m.	4%
6:01 a.m. - 8 a.m.	4%
8:01 a.m. - 10 a.m.	6%
10:01 a.m. - Noon	7%
Total P.M. hours	61%
12:01 p.m. - 2 p.m.	10%
2:01 p.m. - 4 p.m.	9%
4:01 p.m. - 6 p.m.	8%
6:01 p.m. - 8 p.m.	9%
8:01 p.m. - 10 p.m.	14%
10:01 p.m. - Midnight	12%
Not reported	0%

Table 3 – Hours When Officers are Killed

This reveals the need for training for your self defense in low-light conditions. Tactics for low-light conditions will be discussed later in the book.

Types of Weapons Used by the Cop Killer

Firearms were used 92.7% of the time by perpetrators who kill officers. All other types of weapons used ranging from knife to vehicle account for only 7.3% of the weapons used by perpetrators, making firearms the weapon of choice for cop killers.

Total firearms	**92.70%**
Handgun	**67.62%**
Rifle	**18.68%**
Shotgun	**6.41%**
Knife or other cutting instrument	**0.89%**
Bomb	**0.18%**
Blunt instrument	**0.36%**
Personal weapons	**0.36%**
Vehicle	**5.52%**

Table 4 – Cop Killer Weapon Use

Handguns are the most prevalent type of firearm used by perpetrators to kill police officers, accounting for 67.62% of officer deaths.

The following table provides information on the type/size of handgun used by perpetrators to kill officers. Notice that the most likely calibers used correspond to the types of firearms carried by law enforcement, indicating the perpetrators are at least as well armed as law enforcement, and in many cases better armed.

Size of Handgun Ammunition		
Size	**Incidents**	**%**
9 Millimeter	106	20.35%

Size of Handgun Ammunition (continued)		
Size	Incidents	%
.40 Caliber	59	11.32%
.38 Caliber	47	9.02%
.45 Caliber	41	7.87%
.380 Caliber	32	6.14%
.357 Caliber	21	4.03%
.22 Caliber	19	3.65%
.357 Magnum	11	2.11%
.32 Caliber	10	1.92%
.25 Caliber	9	1.73%
Not reported	9	1.73%
.44 Magnum	6	1.15%
10 Millimeter	4	0.77%
.44 Caliber	2	0.38%
.50 Caliber	2	0.38%
.41 Magnum	1	0.19%
7.62x25 Millimeter	1	0.19%

Table 5 – Cop Killer Handgun Caliber

Also note that the 9 millimeter accounts for the vast majority of the weapon calibers preferred by cop killers. It is safe to say that this is the most popular caliber of handgun round today.

Distance of Encounter

Eighty percent of deadly encounters happen within 20 feet distance separating the victim officer and perpetrator. A full 50% of encounters happen at five feet or less. Many of today's firearm courses are fired at multiple distances ranging from three yards to as many as fifty yards. State mandated qualification courses of fire for law enforcement have officers firing the majority of rounds from greater than seven yards (21 feet) and the nearest point of fire is three yards (nine feet) when in actuality the majority of deadly encounters occur within five feet (1.6 yards). The following graphically displays the distances involved in the case of officers killed.

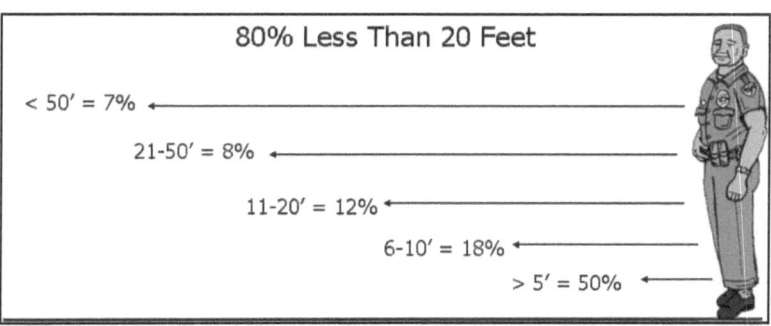

80% Less Than 20 Feet

< 50' = 7%

21-50' = 8%

11-20' = 12%

6-10' = 18%

> 5' = 50%

Figure 3 – Distance of Encounters Where Officers are Murdered

As you can see, fifty percent of deadly encounters occur within five feet separating the slain officer and the perpetrator. Eighteen percent occur between six and ten feet. Twelve percent take place between 11 and 20 feet, while only eight percent occur between 21 and 50 feet. Only seven percent of officer deaths occur when there is a distance between the officer and perpetrator of over 50 feet.

Wound Location

Wound location on those officers killed is important to note because it tells us about the skill of the offender as it pertains to the accuracy of their shots. It also tells us what areas of our bodies we should attempt to protect when facing an aggressor in a future deadly force encounter. The following figure identifies the critical wound location of the officers slain in the line of duty. For those officers killed who were not wearing body armor, 49% of the fatal wounds were to both the torso and the head, while only two percent of officers killed were hit below the waist.

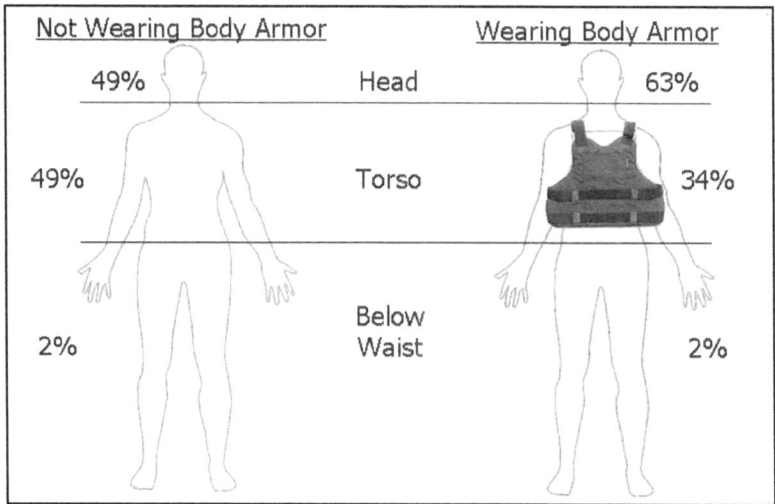

Figure 4 – Wound Locations of Officers Slain

Officers who were wearing body armor had more wounds to the head. This is indicative of the body armor influencing where cop killers placed their shots.

I am a little surprised that those officers who were killed while not wearing body armor had the critical wound in the head 49% of the time. Most likely the underlying data would reveal that the officer actually suffered a center mass hit to the torso, and the cop killer moved closer to the officer and fired a final shot into the head.

From the statistics, it appears that cop killers are fairly accurate at close range and assume that officers are wearing body armor. They further reveal the need for the use of cover and movement when engaged in a deadly force scenario. Both of these points will be covered later in the book.

CIVILIAN CONFRONTATION STATISTICS

While statistics are not kept on armed confrontation in civilian self defense situations, the UCR does provide insight as to what a victim and what a perpetrator may look like.

Victim demographics are not available for all violent crime categories – only for murder victims. The typical murder victim is a black male. Black murder victims account for 49.3% and white murder victims account for 46.8% of the total. Males account for 78.3% of all murder victims. Eighty-seven percent of all murder victims are over the age of 18.

All categories of violent crime are accounted for with regard to suspect information. Violent criminal information is provided below:

Violent Crime Suspect	
Characteristic	**%**
Male	81.7%
White	58.9%
Black	39.0%
Over 18 Years Old	83.7%
18 to 44 Years Old	71.0%
Weapons Used:	
Firearms	68.0%
Knife	12.1%
Personal Weapons (hands, fists, feet, etc.)	5.80%

Table 6 – Violent Crime Suspect Information

Murder suspects are male 81.7% of the time. White suspects account for 58.9% of the total, while black suspects are 39% of the total. A typical murder suspect will be over the age of 18 (83.7% of the time) with the largest majority ranging in age from 18 to 44 years old (71%). The most likely murder weapon is a firearm (68%), followed by a knife or other cutting instrument (12.1%). Personal weapons such as hands, fists, feet, elbows, knees, etc. account for 5.8% of the weapons to commit murder.

As you can see, there is no typical profile of a violent criminal. But as an observant person determined to defend yourself and others, you should focus your skeptical outlook on males between the ages of 18 and 44 years old. Do not let your guard down around strangers fitting this description.

Chapter 4

Defensive Handgun Selection

The best we can hope for concerning the people at large is that they be properly armed.

Alexander Hamilton,
The Federalist Papers

Selecting a defensive handgun is as personal as selecting your brand of toothbrush, toothpaste, clothes, automobile, or any other necessity of life. As a first time defensive handgun purchaser, one must understand and appreciate this fact. Experienced defensive handgunners already know that no one gun fits every person. We are all built differently. Some have large hands, while others have small. Some are larger in stature than are others. Some are stronger, and some are weaker. A defensive handgun should fit you like a well worn pair of jeans. If you are not comfortable, it will not be as effective a tool as it should be.

I use the word "tool" for a reason. The defensive handgun serves one purpose – self defense. With that said, I do not mean that it should never be used outside of self-defense. It should be fired on a regular basis. Go to the range and shoot targets at will. Enter defensive pistol competitions near where you live in order to enhance your comfort with it. Practice drawing, bringing it on target, and dry firing regularly. But when all is said and done, a defensive handgun serves the purpose of self defense!

There is a massive amount of information available on selecting a defensive handgun. Consequently, I will briefly describe the types of weapons that are used as defensive handguns.

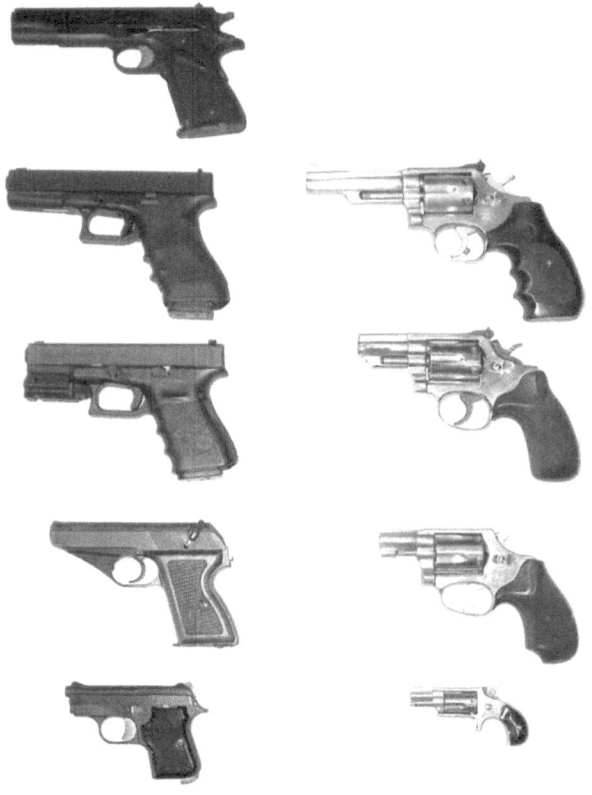

Photo 1 – Semi-Automatic and Revolver

The above photo depicts nine handguns. Semi-automatics on the left from top to bottom include the Colt 1911 Government Model in .45 caliber, Glock 17 9mm, Glock 23 .40 caliber with laser sight, Mauser .380, and at the bottom of the left side is the Armi .25 caliber. The revolvers on the right from top to bottom include the Smith & Wesson Model 66 .357, Model 19 .357, Model 60 .38 caliber, and the North American Arms .22 caliber. These are all weapons I have carried for my personal self defense at one time or another. The two types of handguns – revolvers and semi-automatic pistols are depicted. Each is discussed in more detail in subsequent sections.

Revolvers

Firearms in general were first developed in the 14th century. By the 15th century armies no longer closed in hand-to-hand combat, but rather fought from a distance dictated by the day's firearms. Then, in 1836 Samuel Colt patented the first revolver. Colt's invention led to the saying that "God created man, but Sam Colt made them equal." The handgun has continued to evolve since then.

Revolvers for defensive use can be grouped into three categories – small, medium, and large frame. Only consider double action revolvers viable for defense. The distinction between single and double action revolvers is that with a single action revolver the hammer must be manually pulled back with the thumb in order to cock the weapon. Conversely, double action revolvers can either be cocked by pulling the hammer back like a single action, or you can simply pull the trigger which cocks the hammer for firing.

For defensive handgun and concealed carry purposes, the small and medium frame double action revolvers fit the bill. In my opinion, for defensive purposes, the smallest caliber revolver to consider is the .38 special – more about calibers later in this chapter. This caliber is considered a small frame revolver. Medium framed revolvers are chambered for the .357 magnum, which is more powerful than the .38 caliber and requires more substantial construction to withstand the gas pressures created by the .357 magnum round.

Both small and medium framed revolvers come in 1, 2, 4, and 6 inch barrels. For defensive purposes a four-inch revolver is probably the largest viable weapon, with a two-inch barrel being more preferable because of ease of concealment.

There are numerous manufacturers of small and medium frame revolvers, but I recommend sticking with the better names – Smith & Wesson (S&W), Ruger, Colt – in the business. Each offer excellent choices for a defensive double action revolver. Like automobile manufacturers, gun companies keep introducing new models. Therefore, I will not provide a list of recommended revolvers. Go to your local gun dealer and see what they have in stock, but remember my recommendation on minimum caliber and do not be talked into something smaller than a .38 caliber.

Because of the simplicity of how a double action revolver works, it can be an excellent choice for the novice gun owner as a first defensive handgun.

Semi-Automatic Pistol

Like revolvers, these come in a plethora of calibers and sizes. They, too, can be categorized as small, medium and large frames. The most popular on the market today are the medium frame autoloaders. However, there is another important distinction when talking about semi-automatic pistols and that is the action type. Basically, there are three action types – single action, double/single action, and double action only.

Single Action Semi-Automatic Pistol

John Browning developed this pistol type between 1905 and 1911, and the 1911A1 .45 caliber came to be the United States Military's primary sidearm. The most recognized single action semi-automatic pistol is the Colt 1911 Government Model, which Browning developed. This weapon served the United States Military through World Wars I and II, Korea and Vietnam. It was replaced by the Berretta 92F in 1985, which is known today as the M9.

A single action semi-automatic is similar to the single action revolver in that the hammer must be manually cocked in order to fire the weapon. The hammer is initially cocked when the slide is pulled back and released, chambering a round for firing. However, carrying a single action semi-automatic with the hammer cocked is unsettling for some people.

If the single action semi-automatic pistol does not have a firing pin block, then the hammer cannot be safely let down and carried on a chambered round. This typically leads people to simply not chamber a live round, which then requires that person to manually activate the slide to chamber a round. Unless that person practices religiously doing this manipulation, then it will take too much time to go through this machination in a life or death situation.

Many different calibers can be found today in the single action semi-automatic type of weapon, but the .45 caliber remains the most popular. I love the Colt 1911, but for a number of reasons, I would not recommend this action type as a defense handgun for the first time self defense handgun purchaser.

Double/Single Action Semi-Automatic Pistol

As the name may imply, this action type is a contradiction. It is however, the action type that has dominated new semi-automatic pistols for the past 50 years or so. The contradiction comes from the fact that the first round fired is in double action mode, while the remaining rounds fired are in single action mode. Consequently, the same weapon in essence has two separate and distinct trigger pulls to become accustom to.

A first round is chambered just like the single action semi-auto by inserting a full magazine and pulling the slide to the rear and releasing it to chamber a round. At this point the hammer remains back just like the single action. By rotating the decock safety down, the hammer is dropped on a firing pin block putting the weapon in safe mode.

To fire the first round after the previous sequence for loading and safing the weapon, one must rotate the decock safety upward and simply pull the trigger. However, this first round trigger pull is in double action mode, and most types of these weapons have a very rough, long trigger pull. After the first shot is fired, the blowback of the slide ejects the fired round, moves forward, strips a fresh round out of the magazine, and keeps the hammer cocked. Therefore, the second round fired has a single action trigger pull, which is shorter and smoother than the first double action trigger pull.

From this description, I'm sure you get the point that learning to fire this weapon accurately can take a bit of practice simply from the continuing difference in trigger pull between the first and subsequent rounds fired. Mastering this weapon can indeed be done, but it does take time, commitment, and much practice.

As you can guess, I'm not a big fan of the double/single action semi-automatic pistol. I do own some and was qualified on them before I left law enforcement, but have not fallen in love with this hybrid design for a semi-auto. These weapons do not fit me like a worn pair of jeans.

Putting my bias aside, however, I would not rule these out as viable defensive handguns for someone else. They do offer the advantage of a true safety device, which may be important to many prospective self defenders. Manufacturers of these weapons include Beretta, Ruger, Sig Sauer, Smith & Wesson, and Walther. They come in a wide variety of calibers, but I would not recommend anything less than a 9mm as a serious self-defense semi-automatic pistol.

Double Action Only Semi-Automatic Pistol

This is the newest type of semi-auto pistol. It was introduced in 1982 by Glock. Glock was approached by the Austrian military about building a handgun for them. They wanted to update from the Walther P38 they had been using for decades. Glock designed the Glock 17, named that because it was Gaston Glock's seventeenth patent.

Since then, many manufacturers have introduced pure double action semi-automatic pistols. Kahr, Kimber, Ruger, Smith & Wesson, Springfield Armory, and Walther all offer their own versions of the double action semi-auto pistol.

These firearms fire every time in double action mode. That is you simply pull the trigger and the weapon will fire. Since their introduction, many have overcome their initial reaction to them not having an external, positive safety. However, they all have internal safeties to prevent accidental discharge if dropped, and most have trigger safeties that prevent the weapon from firing if the trigger is not being positively pressed.

Since they are true double action in nature, they make adapting to them as easy as a double action revolver. They became popular in law enforcement in the United States, when most agencies were transitioning to the semi-auto pistol, because retraining officers was easier than with the older double/single action semi-autos.

All of these things are advantages to these action type semi-automatic pistols. This type firearm is my personal choice for a defensive handgun. I own both a Glock 17 (9mm) and a Glock 23 (.40 caliber), carry both on occasion, but prefer the Glock 23 due to the midsize being easier to conceal than the 17 and the added fire power a .40 offers over a 9mm.

CHOOSING THE RIGHT CALIBER FOR YOUR DEFENSE

Over the years there has been much debate about what caliber makes the best defensive handgun round. I have shared my recommendations on what I consider the smallest caliber that I believe to be acceptable as a defensive weapon, but would like to share some of the research that has been conducted over the years in an attempt to arrive at the perfect round.

Let me first say, though, that there is no perfect round. There are advantages and disadvantages to almost all handgun ammunition. If you hit the central nervous system (CNS) with a .22 caliber round, it will stop the threat. If you hit the same threat in the arm with a .45 caliber round, you probably will not stop the threat. Therefore, bullet placement is of prime importance when trying to stop a threat. With that said, regular training with your well fit and comfortable firearm, regardless of caliber, will go a long way to ensure you are able to stop a threat when needed.

Perhaps the single most identifiable incident to have occurred within the last century that formed the debate and subsequent research on stopping power of defensive handguns was the April 11, 1986 FBI Miami Shootout.

Prior to the shootout, the FBI had been investigating several armored car and bank robberies in the Miami area. They had not identified the suspects at that point, but had a description of a Chevrolet Monte Carlo they suspected may be used in a future robbery. Its owner had been found murdered, so they worked on the theory that since vehicles used in prior robberies were stolen that this one may be used.

On that day, a total of eleven FBI agents were conducting surveillance of a number of banks in the same general vicinity that had previously been robbed. Agents had descriptions of the robbery suspects, but no firm identity. While on surveillance, Agents Jerry Dove and Ben Grogan spotted the vehicle they were looking for. It was occupied by two white males that matched the descriptions they had been given. Radio communications informed other agents in the area of the sighting, and federal agents began to attempt to get a marked Miami-Dade unit to perform a vehicle stop.

While all of this was taking place, the suspects became suspicious that they were being followed. The radio log later revealed that the agents reported seeing the suspects loading up their weapons. The suspects began driving down small two-lane streets, but agents waited for a less populated area in which to stop the suspects.

Agents finally reported they were about to perform a felony stop. Dove and Grogan had been joined by other FBI vehicles. While attempting to stop the suspects, agents forced the suspects' vehicle off the road, where it came to rest blocked by a parked car to its right, a tree to its front, Agent Dove and Grogan's vehicle to its rear, and Agent Dick Manauzzi's and Gordon McNeill's vehicle to its left. Another FBI vehicle containing Agents John Hanlon and Edmundo Mireles was across the street from the vehicle stop.

Realizing they were blocked in, the two suspects (William Matix and Michael Platt) opened fire. Matix was armed with a 12 gauge shotgun and got one round off before being wounded, and Platt was armed with a Ruger Mini-14 .223 rifle. Platt's initial rounds were directed at Agents McNeil and Mireles. Both agents were hit – Mireles was wounded in the left arm, disabling his use of it, and McNeil was shot through the right hand. McNeil was able to fire his weapon (a Smith & Wesson Model 19 .357 loaded with .38 +P ammunition) six times. Two of McNeil's rounds struck Matix, rendering him unconscious. Matix fired no more rounds during the confrontation.

Another FBI vehicle, occupied by Agents John Risner and Gilbert Orrantia, arrived on scene. They stopped their vehicle approximately sixty feet to the northwest of the gunfight. They brought Platt under fire from behind the cover of their vehicle.

Platt, realizing he was in a crossfire situation, exited his vehicle and began to advance on the FBI vehicle behind him. He was shooting and moving, armed with the Ruger Mini-14. During his movement, he was struck by two 9mm rounds – one fired by Agent Dove and the other by Agent Risner. Agent Dove's round drove into Platt's lung, while Agent Risner's round hit Platt underneath the armpit. However, he continued his assault on the FBI vehicle being used for cover by Agents Dove and Grogan.

During this assault, Platt continued to fire at agents and struck Agent McNeil again in the neck, paralyzing this agent. Shots fired at Risner and Orrantia resulted in Orrantia being struck by shrapnel and debris produced by one of the .223's near hit on the vehicle. Platt moved on toward Dove and Grogan's position.

Reaching Dove and Grogan's vehicle, Platt flanked them and first shot Grogan and then Dove. Grogan was killed from a gunshot wound to the chest, and Dove died from two rounds to the head. After neutralizing these two agents, Platt got into Dove/Grogan's vehicle and attempted to leave the scene. At this time Matix regained consciousness, rushed to Platt's position, and got into the passenger door to leave with him.

However, the fight was not over for Agent Mireles. Recall he was initially wounded in the left arm, rendering it useless. But he continued to fight. Retrieving a 12 gauge shotgun, Agent Mireles racked a round in the chamber, steadied the barrel on the vehicle bumper, and fired. He continued racking rounds in and firing until he had emptied the shotgun (five rounds total fired). At some point, Platt was wounded in the feet by shotgun pellets. Realizing someone was preventing his escape, Platt got out of the vehicle he was trying to escape in, crossed to Mireles position, and fired three rounds at Mireles. Miraculously, Platt's rounds missed Mireles, but Platt was unaware and returned to the FBI vehicle to leave.

Mireles retrieved his service revolver (Smith & Wesson Model 19 .357 loaded with .38 +P ammunition) and advanced on Platt and Matix, firing as he went. He ultimately unloaded his revolver, killing both suspects.

At the conclusion of the firefight, there were two dead FBI agents, six wounded FBI agents, two dead suspects, and one uninjured FBI agent. The FBI report on the incident states there were a total of 131 identifiable rounds fired, with as many as a total of 140-145 rounds being fired. FBI agents fired a total of 69 rounds, Matix fired one round, and

Platt fired at least 61 rounds. Of the 69 rounds fired by the FBI agents, a total of 18 hit their target (Matix was shot six times and Platt was hit 12 times), which amounts to a 26% hit ratio. While this ratio may seem low, other studies of officer involved shootings reveal that it was actually higher than those other studies revealed. What this should tell us as defensive handgunners is that we need to practice. If trained law enforcement officers have a hit ratio of 26% or less, then we need to increase our practice time so we can be equally, if not more successful when faced with a self defense situation.

A subsequent medical examiner, following the autopsy of Platt, stated that the round fired into Platt's lung by Agent Dove was a fatal wound that would have eventually killed Platt even if he had received immediate medical treatment, but as you know it did not stop Platt from killing two FBI agents and trying to drive away.

Subsequent investigation revealed that both Matix and Platt were former military men – Matix was a military policemen and Platt was former Special Forces. Platt's training was obvious during this shootout. It should also be noted, that both Matix and Platt's toxicology reports came back clean – neither had any drugs or alcohol in their systems at the time of this gun battle. They were just not willing to give up or quit.

As one can imagine, this shootout and the resultant information about the number of hits that each suspect took, resulted in the FBI relooking its weapon and ammunition selection. What weapons and ammo were used by the FBI during this shootout? Agents armed with revolvers were carrying the Smith & Wesson Model 19 .357 loaded with 158 grain Jacketed Hollow Point (JHP) .38 caliber +P ammunition, while the agents carrying the 9mm were using the Smith & Wesson Model 459 loaded with 115 grain Hollow Point (HP) silver tip ammunition.

During the subsequent study of this shootout and the weapons and ammo used, the Unit Chief of the FBI Firearms

Training Unit told a gun writer that, "all other things aside, Miami was an ammunition failure." The Deputy Unit Chief went further in a document entitled "10mm Notes," by writing, "Dove made a perfect shot, the gun worked perfectly, the bullet failed to do what was necessary. Had the bullet met currently established FBI standards, Platt's heart would have been penetrated and he could have lasted 30 seconds or so - not the four minutes plus after which he killed Grogan and Dove."

In order to determine the best defensive handgun ammo, one must first understand the mechanics of the factors playing a part in wound effectiveness. In July 1989 the FBI Firearms Training Unit issued a report entitled, "Handgun Wounding Factors and Effectiveness." This FBI report drew heavily on research done by Dr. Martin L. Fackler of the Letterman Army Institute of Research, who issued a report entitled, "What's Wrong with the Wound Ballistics Literature, and Why" in July 1987. I will share some of the conclusions of both these reports in our quest for determining the best defensive handgun round possible.

Handgun Ammunition Incapacitating Characteristics

When a human target is hit by a handgun round there are four characteristics identifiable – penetration, permanent cavity, temporary cavity and fragmentation.

1. Penetration

   Penetration is the distance or depth the round travels inside the human body. In order to hit a vital organ from the side, which may require the projectile to penetrate an arm first, it must travel 10 to 12 inches to pass through the heart. Shooting front on into the abdomen, the round must penetrate approximately seven inches in a slender body to reach the major blood vessels in the abdominal cavity.

2. Permanent Cavity

Permanent cavity is the hole left by the bullet penetration into the body. This hole is produced by the bullet cutting and tearing tissue as it bores into the body. Permanent cavity is a result of the penetration depth and the frontal area of the bullet. Simple conclusion, the bigger the bullet, when penetration occurs, results in a larger permanent cavity.

3. Temporary Cavity

This temporary cavity occurs when tissue is pushed aside as the bullet penetrates the body. As the name implies, it is temporary. The human body is very elastic and resilient in nature. Much store was put into temporary cavity in a 1970s study conducted for the Law Enforcement Assistance Administration entitled, "Relative Incapacitation Index." It has since been invalidated. The fact of the matter is that temporary cavity plays no part in incapacitation of a person receiving a gunshot wound.

4. Fragmentation

Fragmentation occurs when the bullet breaks apart as it is traveling into the body. Secondary fragmentation occurs as bone is broken and projected along with the bullet away from the permanent cavity. Fragmentation occurs a significant percent of the time in rifle bullets, but is much less prevalent with handgun ammunition. The primary difference is that rifle bullet velocities can exceed 2000 feet per second; whereas, handgun ammunition generally does not exceed 1400-1500 feet per second. Therefore, one cannot rely on handgun round fragmentation as a primary incapacitating factor in defensive uses.

There are ammunition manufacturers who have developed bullets designed to fragment. The most notable is the Glaser Safety Slug. When Dr. Fackler was asked how long it would take someone to die who had been shot with the Glaser Safety Slug in the front mid-abdomen, he promptly said, "About three days, and the cause of death would be peritonitis (acute inflammation caused by invasion of bacterial matter or a foreign object)."

Much has been written over the years regarding "knockdown" and "stopping" power of a handgun. For the most part these are mythical terms when the unpredictable nature of a human target is taken into account. First let us look at knockdown power.

Technically there is no such thing as knockdown power. Pure physics dictate that for every action there is equal reaction. Therefore, in order for a bullet from a handgun to be able to knock a grown man down when hit by it, then the person who fired it would equally be knocked down by the recoil delivered as the bullet left the barrel of the gun. We know this simply does not occur, so the physical impact of the bullet into a human body is no greater than the felt recoil from the weapon firing that bullet. Of course this does not take into account any psychological effects of being shot. Many people may be preconditioned to fall down upon being hit from a bullet, but in more cases than not, when a person is in the heat of battle, they may not even know they have been shot until after the gun battle is over.

Stopping power implies that a handgun round has the ability to stop an aggressor simply by hitting that aggressor. This too is a fallacy. The only sure way of stopping an aggressor in their tracks is by a well placed shot into the central nervous system (e.g., brain and spinal column). Since defensive marksmen are trained to shoot at center mass, the odds of striking someone in the head or the spinal column are remote. And during the heat of battle, accurate shots are of a premium. Recall the 26% hit ratio of the

Miami Shootout. Consequently, the only other way to incapacitate an aggressor is to cause massive bleeding from the internal organs and blood vessels, causing circulatory collapse, and this takes time. A human being can continue to act for 10-15 seconds even after a shot through the heart.

With this said, only two of the previous factors will determine the outcome of a defensive handgun encounter, and they are penetration and permanent cavity. The FBI recommendation is that a bullet must penetrate 12-18 inches of soft body tissue to be considered effective in incapacitating an aggressor. Anything less than 12 inch penetration is considered unreliable for a defensive handgun round.

The second factor – permanent cavity – as previously defined is the size of the hole. Most ammunition manufacturers have designed their defensive handgun rounds to expand upon impact. Expansion simply increases the size of the hole, but expansion without penetration is also ineffective. Also like fragmentation, expansion does not always occur. What this suggests is that larger diameter bullets begin with a bigger cross section – thus creating a larger permanent cavity than a smaller caliber round. This is why the .45 caliber round is so liked by defensive handgunners. However, this should not predispose someone against a smaller caliber weapon than a .45.

Disagreement continued after the ground breaking research that the FBI, assisted by Dr. Fackler, did because Dr. Fackler's conclusions, as were the FBI's, were based on testing ammunition against ballistic gelatin and not against human bodies. Many gun writers questioned the applicability of the testing since the study of human gunshot wounds did not occur. However, in 1991 Eugene Wolberg published a study in the "Journal of the International Wound Ballistics Association" entitled, "Performance of the Winchester 9mm 147 Grain Subsonic Jacketed Hollow Point Bullet in Human Tissue and Tissue Simulant." Mr. Wolberg was the Senior Firearms Criminologist at the San Diego

Police Crime Laboratory, and he had compiled data on human gunshot wounds inflicted by officers of the San Diego Police Department.

San Diego Police Department adopted the 9mm 147 grain Winchester Subsonic Jacketed Hollow Point (JHP) for its officers in 1987. Mr. Wolberg's data was compiled during autopsies of 27 criminals shot by police officers. Typically, medical examiners do not measure penetration or expansion during autopsies, but Mr. Wolberg requested that this data be captured and the medical examiner honored the request. Only shots that remained in the body were measured for this study.

What Mr. Wolberg found was that average penetration depth for this round in human tissue was 13 inches, and the average expansion ratio was 1.15. When compared to Dr. Fackler's gelatin tests for the same Winchester round, which resulted in an average penetration of 13 inches and an expansion ratio of 1.20, then one can conclude that Dr. Fackler's gelatin test results are consistent with that found in human tissue.

With this background, the following are my recommendations on what round you should carry in your defensive handgun. I make my recommendations based on the two factors previously mentioned as being the two most important – penetration and permanent cavity. Determining permanent cavity was based on recovered expansion of the recommended bullet. There are many rounds that could be recommended. Some penetrate deeper than these listed, but may not expand as much as these listed. Based on these criteria, I recommend the following rounds:

Caliber	Name of Load	Bullet Weight (grains)	Muzzle Velocity (fps)	Penetration Depth (inches)	Expanded Diameter (inches)	Wound Volume (cubic inches)
38	CCI/Speer GD	88	914	17.2"	0.35"	1.66cu
38	Fed HydraShok	90	971	12.0"	0.49"	2.26cu
9x19	Fed HydraShok	147	995	15.6"	0.60"	4.41cu
9x19	Win Ranger Talon	147	1017	15.5"	0.65"	5.14cu
10mm	Norma	170	1358	17.0"	0.63"	5.30cu
10mm	Win Black Talon	200	901	15.6"	0.67"	5.50cu
357SIG	CCI/Speer GD	125	1372	19.1"	0.54"	4.36cu
357MAG	Fed JHP	158	1200	15.9"	0.64"	5.12cu
40SW	Rem G.S.	180	954	14.8"	0.67"	5.20cu
40SW	Win Ranger PG	165	1109	14.5"	0.72"	5.90cu
45ACP	Fed Hi-Shok	230	860	17.4"	0.67"	6.13cu
45ACP	Rem G.S.	230	871	18.9"	0.73"	7.89cu

Table 7 – Recommended Defensive Handgun Ammunition

Note that nothing smaller than a .38 caliber is listed. As I previously stated, anything smaller than a .38 caliber is unreliable in my opinion for defensive work. Also, understand that wound volume is the size of the wound channel in cubic inches calculated for each load by multiplying the average frontal surface area of the recovered bullets by the average depth of penetration.

Concealed Carry Holster Selection

There are many types of holsters that can be used for concealed carry. There are shoulder, inside the waistband, pancake, cross draw, retention, ankle, molded, leather, fanny pack, and a host of other holsters you can carry. These again will be selected on a basis of fit. Are you a small or large person? What is the typical weather like where you will be carrying? Do you normally wear a coat, vest or sweater? Can you be comfortable with a gun in your waistband? These types of questions all come into play when selecting your perfect conceal carry rig.

Keep in mind that circumstances will dictate to some degree what holster best suits you. For example, during the winter when I wear a coat, I carry a Fobus paddle holster. It can easily be concealed under a coat and does a great job of supporting my weapons. An additional bonus is that the CL2 Model I have can hold either my Glock 17 or 23. Since I live in Georgia and the summers are very hot and muggy and I tend to wear shorts and tee shirts mostly, I carry a fanny pack holster during the summer. Therefore, personal circumstances will dictate what holster is best for you.

Many fine holster manufacturers exist. Simply Google your search terms and review the descriptions and reviews of the products you are interested in. Many times holsters can be purchased more inexpensively over the internet than at your local gun store simply because many internet marketers do not have a physical store – thus having lower overhead requirements.

Bottom Line Selection Criteria

Selecting your defensive handgun and concealed carry rig is a personal preference. Do not buy the first one you look at. Do not buy the one the sales person recommends. Buy only the one that will fit you like a well worn pair of jeans. This means you most likely will want to fire the weapon you are contemplating purchasing. Most indoor pistol ranges, and some outdoor ranges, have weapons for rent. If you have one of these in your area, go rent the guns you are looking at buying and try them out. Make sure they fit your hand, have controllable recoil, and are concealable. Then you will be making a knowledgeable purchase, and one you can live with for years to come.

Chapter 5

Firearms Safety

We hoped by this time that the standard rules of safe gun handling would have become universal throughout the world. They have been arrived at by careful consideration over the years, and they do not need modification or addition.

Jeff Cooper

Gun safety has been around since the first gun was invented. I am sure there were accidental discharges in the early years, and like all else in our evolution as humans, we make rules based on experience. These rules have been handed down in order to protect the species, as have thousands of other rules.

Gun safety is a mindset, however, not just a set of rules to memorize. One must acquire the mindset, live it, preach it, and demand that it be followed at all times by all people. Just because someone may be considered an expert marksman does not relieve that person from following basic firearms safety rules. Or just because a person is a law enforcement officer does not mean they no longer have to follow the rules of safe gun handling. You get the point – gun safety is the responsibility of all who handle guns.

GUN SAFETY COMMANDMENTS

As I previously mentioned, Jeff Cooper is known as the father of modern pistol technique. In becoming recognized as this, Colonel Cooper developed four basic rules of firearms safety that hold relevance today. These four rules are more than just rules. I consider them to be commandments!

1. All guns are always loaded.
2. Never let the muzzle cover anything you are not willing to destroy.
3. Keep your finger off the trigger until your sights are on the target.
4. Identify your target, and what is behind it.

All Guns Are Always Loaded

This is a simple concept to grasp. ALL GUNS ARE ALWAYS LOADED! If you develop this mindset, you should never have an accidental discharge. If everyone subscribes to this concept, then accidental discharge and death by firearm can be prevented. It is truly a mindset that everyone should strive to maintain. Failure to do so can lead to serious disasters.

I am reminded of three incidents that I have personal knowledge of. As a police officer, I was the leader of one of my department's Special Weapons and Tactics (SWAT) teams. One of my former team members left the department to go to work at the local Sheriff's Department, where he joined their SWAT team. Their team had been out training one day. They had been conducting building clearing scenarios. During the scenarios, all participants had unloaded weapons and a rigorous weapons check was conducted prior to the training beginning to ensure no live ammunition was being introduced into the scenario area. The training session went well without any injuries or accidental discharges.

After training was completed, the SWAT team members left the training area and returned to the squad room at the precinct. Officers had driven either their agency or personal vehicles to the remote training area, so they all reloaded their Smith & Wesson autoloaders on their way back to the precinct.

When they arrived they went into the squad room to debrief the day's training. During this debriefing, my former team member had his feet propped up on a desk. He pulled his pistol out, aimed at his big toe, and was going to dry fire his weapon. What a surprise he got when the weapon discharged, hitting him in the big toe.

Fortunately, he did not sustain any permanent damage, but he did require medical treatment and missed time off from work. Unfortunately, he has lived the last 30 years with this incident hanging over him. On a positive note, the local firemen got a laugh out of his accident; whereas, they coined a new term for the SWAT acronym – Shoot Weapon at Toe.

Another incident happened during shift change in my squad room. A fellow officer had just gotten a new revolver that he was carrying that night for the first time. Another officer asked to see his new weapon and the officer un-holstered and handed the other officer the revolver. The officer who had asked to see the revolver promptly raised it up, sited at the front wall, and attempted to dry fire the weapon. It discharged, penetrating the front wall, entered the locker room and lodged in a locker. Again, fortunately no one was injured, and the offending officer was thoroughly embarrassed.

The third incident happened, again at the local Sheriff's Department, where an officer had just gotten a new assault rifle. Another officer asked to see it, at which time he promptly shouldered it, aimed at a nearby power transformer on a telephone pole, and pulled the trigger. The shot punctured the transformer, knocking out power to the surrounding area. This officer, also, was very embarrassed by the incident, but fortunately again, no one was injured.

These examples highlight the need for internalizing the mindset that All Guns Are Always Loaded. Because if trained police officers can have accidental discharges, so can anyone else.

Actions that you should take in following this rule include:

- When someone hands you a weapon, always remove the rounds. If you get in the habit of opening the cylinder of a revolver and removing the rounds, you and everyone around you will be safe. Or when handed an autoloader, you always remove the magazine and pull the slide back and lock it to the rear, you and everyone else will be safe.

- When you hand someone a gun, you should always remove the ammunition, or check for ammunition, before handing that person the weapon.

- When at your local gun store or gun show and you ask to see a weapon, you always check whether it is loaded.

- When carrying a weapon from one point to another that is not being used for self defense, without having it properly secured, it should always be unloaded.

- When storing a weapon you do not plan on using in self-defense, it should always be stored unloaded.

- ALL GUNS ARE ALWAYS LOADED!!!!

Never Let The Muzzle Cover Anything You Are Not Willing To Destroy

Another relatively simple concept to understand is this one. It means you never point your gun at anything you are not willing to kill. This includes you. When we discuss defensive techniques and tactics we will be addressing issues of draw, fire and move. It is easy to inadvertently cross parts of your body with the muzzle if you are not conscious of where the muzzle is pointed.

A part of defensive handgun practice includes practicing drawing and firing exercises that can be done at your home when you cannot get to a range, but this is done after ensuring the weapon is unloaded. However, it does not include pointing your weapon at other people or animals. The muzzle of the firearm should never be directed at anything you are not willing to hit in any circumstance.

Keep Your Finger Off The Trigger Till Your Sights Are On Target

When handling a firearm, your trigger finger should always be indexed along the side of the firearm's frame. This is called indexing. It should be practiced always. Even when we are in a gunfight where we are shooting and moving, the trigger finger should be indexed when we are not on target and actively pressing the trigger to deliver accurate fire against our target.

Most defensive holsters are designed to where indexing is a natural thing when drawing from the holster. It is easy to maintain this index until the weapon is up and the sights are on target.

Instilling this concept into your mindset will ensure that the always loaded handgun is never accidentally fired!

Identify Your Target And What Is Behind It

Recall the 26% hit ratio from the Miami Shootout. More than 100 rounds were fired, 69 from the FBI agents. Bad guys do not have to follow this rule, but law enforcement and the innocent citizen acting in self defense better. If you don't know what you are shooting at, chances are you won't hit it. Firing at noises in home defense could result in your shooting a family member, which would be disastrous.

What is behind the known target is also of concern. When acting in self-defense on the street, you most likely will be in an area occupied by other innocent people. A stray round from your weapon could injure or kill an innocent person, which would also be disastrous.

A prime example of why knowing your target and what is behind it is so important is one that happened in my agency after I had left the department. Detectives where looking for a serial rapist. They received information from a confidential informant that the suspect could be found at a certain house at a specific address. Acting on this information, detectives coordinated with patrol, and three patrol officers approached the door to the house while detectives set up on the back door.

The patrol officers knocked on the door at approximately 1:00 a.m. and there was no answer. Several attempts to get someone to the door went unanswered, at which time the detectives directed the patrol officers to kick in the door. Their legal justification was based on their having an arrest warrant for the serial rapist and the information provided by the confidential informant.

Following orders, the patrol officers kicked in the door and entered into the living room. The first two officers in performed a good, tactical door entry. As the third officer was entering, shots were fired from the end of the hallway. These rounds impacted the door frame next to the third officer, who fell back onto the porch. The two officers who had already entered thought their partner had been hit and returned fire down the hallway until the incoming rounds ceased.

When all the firing was over, the officers found a sixty something year old male critically wounded, and his wife sitting in bed screaming. As it turned out, the critically wounded man died, and it was determined that he had no idea who was breaking into his house. In his mind he was defending his home and wife. The officers thought that the suspect they were looking for was firing at them and had already hit one of their brother officers when they returned fire. As it was, this was a seriously unfortunate accident because the serial rapist was not there and the homeowners had never heard of him.

None of the officers involved were prosecuted. However, all five officers involved are now no longer in law enforcement. They each left on their own to pursue other employment. And the city paid a huge sum of money to settle the civil case out of court.

I will not attempt to justify or discuss the legalities of this incident. However, I will point out that had the homeowner and the police officers have followed this rule on Identifying Your Target, this may not have turned out to be such a tragic incident.

There are numerous variations of these commandments, but they all effectively mean the same thing. I have found these four to be succinct and direct without belaboring the need to practice firearms safety. Read them, understand them, and instill them into your mindset and you should never experience an accidental discharge.

RANGE SAFETY RULES

Each range complex has their own set of range rules unique to them. All, however, will cover the same major points. The following is a set of generic range rules to familiarize readers with what to expect.

- Know and obey all range commands.
- Know your weapon.
- Only authorized weapons are allowed.
- Only use recommended ammunition.
- All firing will be allowed only from designated firing positions.
- No loading or unloading of firearms except in designated areas.
- Keep action open with muzzle pointed downrange when not firing.
- Do not load your weapon until on the firing line.
- Eye and ear protection are required when firing.
- Be aware of where others are.

- Only authorized targets (e.g., paper or metal) are allowed – no bottles or cans.
- Open, unload and secure firearms during cease fire.
- No glass of any kind permitted on the range.
- Do not handle firearms or stand on the firing line while others are downrange.
- No smoking, eating or drinking on the firing line.
- No fully automatic weapons allowed.
- No alcoholic beverages allowed on range.
- Remove all targets and debris when finished.
- Always practice safety on the range.
- Notify the range manager of any injuries.
- No horseplay or unsafe firearms use will be allowed.
- When shooting metal targets, maintain a safe distance of at least 10 feet to prevent splash back of the bullet fragments.
- All firing is limited to down range within the range confines.
- Do not step off the firing line, turn to the side, or turn around while the line is "hot," unless instructed to do so.
- Ensure that the weapon is not cocked, and fingers are outside the trigger guard when holstering a weapon.
- Do not step forward to pick up items dropped while the line is "hot." Wait until the line is called safe and instructed to do so.
- If a weapon is dropped, let it fall. Do not attempt to catch it.

This list is not all inclusive of possible safety rules, but do contain what you can expect to see on most ranges within the United States. Be aware that each range will have its own set of rules, so be familiar with and follow them!

HOME FIREARMS SAFETY

As a gun owner and perhaps a parent, you have a responsibility to keep your firearms out of reach of children and others that you have not specifically authorized access to them. As a defensive handgun owner, you have a responsibility to your family and yourself to be prepared to protect them. Therefore, you will need to be able to safely store a loaded handgun in order to meet both responsibilities.

If you only own a self defense handgun, loaded weapon storage is a must. However, the handgun must be easily accessible as well. A product I recommend for defensive handgun safe storage is the GunVault. Information on this line of products can be found at:

http://www.gunvault.com/home.nxg

GunVault makes models that utilize their No-Eyes® Keypad technology and a biometric locking mechanism. All of their products are designed for the safe storage of a defensive handgun, while providing immediate access when needed.

For those of you who, like I, own multiple weapons there are safety rules that need to be abided by in the home. The following is a list of what I believe needs to occur in the home to keep unauthorized people, including children, from gaining access to your firearms.

- Never store a gun loaded, with the exception of your safely stored defensive handgun.
- Guns should be locked in a cabinet, closet, safe or other controllable location that prevents access. Do not leave the key in the locks or give combinations to young children.
- If unable to lock guns away, then install gun locks on all weapons. There are basically two types of individual gun locks – trigger and cable locks. Both work well at preventing weapon manipulation. If using a trigger lock, ensure the weapon is unloaded. Cable locks actually go through frames preventing introduction of ammunition.

- Ammunition should be stored under lock separate from firearms.

Home gun safety is a common sense proposition. Do not tempt young ones by leaving guns loaded and accessible. Your kids know how to open drawers, crawl in closets, and climb up clothes to get to closet shelves, so none of these hiding places are acceptable without gun locks being installed on empty weapons!

TEACHING CHILDREN FIREARMS SAFETY

In 1902 Mark Beaufoy, a British sportsman, presented his young son with a shotgun as a present. Along with the shotgun, he presented the following poem that he had written on gun safety.

A Father's Advice
Mark Beaufoy, 1902

Never, never let your gun
Pointed be at anyone;
That it may unloaded be
Matters not the least to me

When a hedge or fence you cross,
Though of time it cause a loss,
From your gun the cartridge take
For the greater safety sake.

If 'twixt you and neighbouring gun
Bird may fly or beast may run,
Let this maxim e'er be thine:
'Follow not across the line.'

Stops and beaters, oft unseen,
Lurk behind some leafy screen;

Calm and steady always be;
'Never shoot where you can't see'

Keep your place and silent be;
Game can hear and game can see;
Don't be greedy, better spared
Is a pheasant, than one shared.

You may kill or you may miss,
But at all times think of this -
'All the pheasants ever bred
Won't repay for one man dead.

If you read the poem carefully, you will notice the similarities of what is being said to the previous commandments and rules I presented on gun safety. These lessons are time honored and have been passed from generation to generation. If you have small children growing up in a home with guns present, it is your responsibility to teach them how to use a gun safely.

When is a good time to do that? I have three children and all are of different personalities. In fact, sometimes I wonder how the three of them came from the same parents because they are so different, but then at other times they do things the same. With my two boys, obviously toy guns played a part in their younger play days. This is an excellent age to begin talking to them about gun safety. Teach them the same four commandments previously discussed.

As they get older, it is alright to introduce them to real guns. My sons were around eight years old when I took them out and taught them how to fire a .22 rifle. My youngest son regularly competes with me at local International Defense Pistol Association (IDPA) matches. Both my sons have a healthy respect for guns, just as I was taught by my father.

My daughter is seven and has already shown a curiosity about guns. She sees her brothers and me cleaning them after a day at the range. I do not discourage her curiosity, but rather encourage it and use it as an opportunity to teach her about gun safety. I will let her hold the gun after I've cleaned it. There is nothing wrong with this. This is how I was taught at a young age. Children are naturally curious, so do not try to hide the gun or not let them touch it because this will only breed further curiosity. But the whole time you are allowing them to touch the gun you remind them that it is not a toy, that it could hurt them or someone else very badly, and that they must never touch a gun unless you are around.

My daughter is already asking me to take her shooting, which I will do at about the same age as I did with her brothers.

While teaching your own children to respect guns and to be safe with them is your responsibility, the National Rifle Association (NRA) has a very good child gun safety program entitled Eddie Eagle GunSafe® Program, which is for children that are perhaps too young to put through a regular NRA training course.

The essence of this course can be summed up by the four steps that are taught to the young children in regards to what to do if they find a gun. These fours steps are:

1. STOP!
2. Don't Touch.
3. Leave the Area.
4. Tell an Adult.

Stop and Don't Touch are the two most important points in this list. You do not want your child touching a gun if you are not around. You must impress upon them the importance of following this simple four step process in responsible gun safety.

You should teach your young children these four steps. Turn it into a game by role-playing these steps with your child. Take a picture of a gun, or even a toy gun, and place it in an open area of a room out of sight of your child. Sit your child down and discuss these four points. Then ask your child to go into the room where the gun picture is and tell her that when she finds a gun, to follow the steps. Try to watch what she does while she searches for the gun photograph or toy gun. If she touches the gun, then reinforce the four steps. Continue this role-play until your child completes the four steps. Periodically repeat this to reinforce the idea of what they should do if they ever find a gun.

Gun safety is your responsibility. Instill the four commandments into your psyche and live by them. Properly store your weapons and ammunition, and teach your family to respect firearms. If everyone does this, then accidental firearm deaths can be prevented!

Chapter 6

Defensive Handgun Tactics and Techniques

The purpose of the pistol is to stop a fight that somebody else has started, almost always at very short range.
Jeff Cooper

Being an effective defensive handgun shooter depends on three things – accuracy, power, speed. The following graphically depicts this relationship.

Defensive Handgun Triad

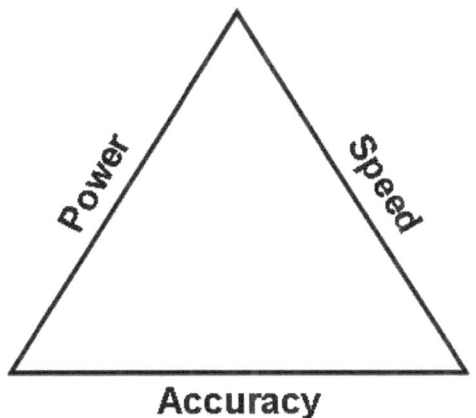

Figure 5 – Defensive Handgun Triad

Notice that the base of the triangle is accuracy. If you cannot hit your target, you will not be effective. Being able to reliably hit your target is essential. If two shooters square off, one shooting a .22 and the other a .45 and the .45 shooter cannot hit their target and the .22 shooter can, the .22 shooter will win the encounter. Strive for accuracy first.

The left side of the triangle is Power. This simply refers to the power of your chosen weapon and ammunition, which we addressed in a previous chapter.

Speed is how fast you can deliver your accurate, powerful shots. Speed comes as accuracy is developed. Do not get frustrated when first starting to shoot if you are not very fast. Continue to practice and the speed will come. How fast is fast enough? The IDPA recommends striving for one accurate shot every one second. You will not start at this rate of fire and be accurate, so you will have to continue to work toward this goal – but accuracy is the foundation!

In order to develop accuracy and speed, one must have a stable shooting platform, which will be discussed next.

Stable Shooting Platform

The most widely used and tactically sound stance is the typical fighting stance – that is, weak side foot slightly forward of the strong side foot. For a right handed shooter this would mean the left foot is slightly forward of the right foot. This stance does several things for you. First it places your weapon away from a potential aggressor, assuming you are wearing a holster on the hip or in the right rear of your back. Second, it provides you with a hand to ward off the attacker or distract them while bringing your weapon to bear. This stance also presents a smaller target to your adversary than would standing completely face on. And finally, it provides the best stance for maintaining balance if your attacker hits, charges, or shoots you.

Both hands should ideally be used to hold your weapon. Two ways of holding your weapon that has wide acceptance is the Weaver and Isosceles stances. In the Weaver stance the weak side is forward. Your weapon is held in your strong hand with your strong arm extended almost straight, while the weak hand is used to support your strong hand. The strong hand is pushing, while the weak hand is pulling, providing a very stable platform by which to shoot from.

The Isosceles stance is where both strong and weak hands and arms are pushed toward the target – the strong hand holding the weapon and the weak hand supporting it. In this stance, the body is square (completely face on) to the target. Looking down from above a shooter employing this technique resembles a triangle that is formed by the body as the base and the two arms as the sides – hence the name "Isosceles" stance. Studies of police officer involved shootings reveal the majority of officers are trained in the Weaver stance, but typically revert to an Isosceles stance when involved in an altercation.

I prefer the Weaver stance because of the reasons previously mentioned – weapon protection, free hand toward attacker, smaller target, maintain balance.

Grip is the function of holding the weapon. The strong hand should be comfortably wrapped around the handle of the handgun, with the weak hand providing a supporting role by wrapping the fingers around the fingers of the strong hand and aligning the weak hand thumb alongside, atop, or under the strong hand thumb. By placing the thumbs in this manner, it ensures the weak hand thumb is not strapped over the strong hand thumb under the slide of a semi-automatic pistol, which could cause injury of the weak hand thumb and interfere with weapon function.

Aligning the sites, or sight alignment, should have the front sight visible equally between the side posts of the rear sight, with the tops of the front sight and rear sights level. The following graphic depicts what the correct sight picture should look like when using a three-dot sight system. Note that the top of the front sight is at the bottom, or six o'clock position, of where you want impact to occur on the target.

Figure 6 – Sight Alignment

Impact on this target would occur in the upper part of the center torso based on this sight alignment. However, in defensive handgun encounters, it may not always be possible to obtain a perfect sight picture. In fact, numerous debriefings of law enforcement officers following deadly force encounters with their handguns, reveal that a vast number of these officers openly admit not being aware of their sights. This leads one to believe that these officers may have relied on point shooting, which could account for the low ratio of hits to rounds fired that was previously mentioned.

There is a technique used in training defensive handgunners called the "flash sight." In firing handguns, because barrels are short, unlike rifles, and defensive handgun encounters are at close range, the more important of the two sights (e.g., front and rear) is the front sight. It is the front sight that ultimately determines where a round will impact a target. If the front sight is set high, the round will impact high, low and the round impacts low, right and the round impacts to the right, and so on. Flash sighting then concentrates on the front sight. When drawing your weapon and bringing it on target, focus on the front sight being placed on the target where you want impact to occur. In the short distances of defensive handgun encounters, this should ensure a hit on the target.

Another useful technique to apply is the turret technique. Consider how the turret of a tank moves when acquiring a target, so should your handgun. As you are scanning, rotate your handgun to cover the area that your eyes are focused on. This will prevent time lag from when a target is acquired and when the weapon is positioned to direct accurate fire on a threat.

Target Engagement

Physiological responses to a violent encounter inhibit eye-hand movement and coordination. As was discussed in Chapter 4, there are two ways of stopping an aggressor – a hit to the central nervous system or hitting internal organs causing massive bleeding. Because of the difficulty hitting the small areas of the central nervous system, defensive handgunners should aim for the center mass of the torso.

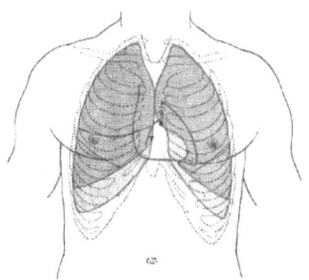

Figure 7 – Center Mass

However, as you will note from studying this figure, center mass would actually be the solar plexus area of the torso. Aiming at this point would actually miss the major organs contained within the ribcage. Consequently, a well placed shot in this area may not stop an attacker's aggression before they can cause death or serous bodily injury to you. The actual aim point should be slightly above center mass (think in line with the arm pits) of the torso to ensure maximum incapacitation of your attacker.

A technique to ensure stopping an attacker is the triple tap. The triple tap is where the defensive handgunner fires two shots to center mass and one shot to the head. Utilizing this technique ensures that two quick shots go to center mass, but realizing that hits in this area may not stop an aggressor for some time, a third shot to the head will. Many violent criminals have begun to wear body armor designed to stop handgun rounds. While hitting someone in the center mass who is wearing body armor will cause impact trauma, it will not necessarily stop that person. A third shot to the head will.

Many teach the triple tap should be performed with two rounds to center mass, a short pause to assess the situation, followed by a third round to the head. Pausing for an assessment may give the aggressor the time to complete their attack on you. For this reason, I do not subscribe to the assess phase of the triple tap. Long ago in martial arts classes, I was taught that if you are hitting someone it should be done in threes. That is, complete three striking maneuvers before backing up and assessing the situation. How many times have you seen a fight where the first person to swing throws one punch and waits to see what effect it has, only to be attacked in response. In a life and death encounter, we do not want to give our attacker the opportunity to hurt or kill us or our loved ones; therefore, triple tap and then assess the situation.

After target engagement and neutralization, remain alert and scan the area to ensure there is no other threat present.

Tactical Priority

Since thugs who commit violent crimes are typically cowardly people, they tend to flock together. Therefore, you may find yourself faced with more than one threat. There may be two or more accomplices with the main antagonizer. In this case, one must be prepared to engage multiple targets. In such a case, how do you determine which to engage first?

Tactical priority is the answer to this question. Simply put, tactical priority dictates that the most dangerous person be engaged first. Dangerousness can be determined by identifying the weaponry of the various threats. A person armed with a shotgun is more dangerous than a person with a knife. However, the person with the knife may be closer than the shotgunner, which may change the dynamics of who is engaged first.

Judgment will ultimately be required by the situation. Who is the most vocal? This will most likely indicate the leader. Thug leaders tend to be the most vocal. Think of the pack mentality displayed by dogs and wild animals. Leaders are both quiet and surrounded by the pack, or are out in front making the most noise. With people, there is little difference from this pack mentality.

Bottom line – which threat do you personally feel most threatened by?

You do need to consider the weaponry and distances involved. The shotgun is obviously the most lethal weapon compared to a knife, but if the knife welding thug is three feet away and the shotgunner is 20 feet away, the knife may be placing you in more jeopardy. If the thug 20 feet away is armed with a handgun and the knife welder is three feet away, the knife represents the most jeopardy again.

It is a judgment call. However, technically speaking when it comes to tactical priority it means to take the most heavily armed threat first and work down to the least heavily armed.

Low Light Accessories

Recall from Chapter 3 that the majority of law enforcement deadly force encounters occur during low light or darkness. There is no reason to believe that civilian use of force incidents occur any less frequently during low light or darkness. With this the case, one must prepare for low light encounters. There are a number of weapon sights and accessories designed to improve accuracy in low light conditions. Furthermore, there are a number of flashlight techniques that can be used to ensure safety and accuracy of the shooter.

What are night sights? Night sights are self illuminating sights that replace most stock front and rear sights. There are several on the market made by different manufacturers. In low light conditions they allow one to draw their weapon and get it on target much quicker than non-illuminated sights allow – and as you know by now, speed is necessary to be successful in a defensive handgun encounter. As stated, there are many manufactures including Ameriglo®, Meprolight®, Trijicon®, and Truglo®. My personal favorite, however, is XS Systems 24/7 Express Big Dot sight.

The Big Dot sight is so called because of the larger area of the front sight than is normally found on front sights. The front sight blade is no larger, only the dot on the front sight. The rear sight is a dove tail type sight, unlike the standard square notches found on typical rear sights. Also, the rear sight illumination is a simple vertical post. As the manufacturer states, the process of sight alignment is nothing more than "dot the i." That is, you simply align the Big Dot front sight to sit over the top of the vertical post of the rear sight. This sight is one of the fastest, if not the fastest, sight to get on target. In the dark, with this sight, there is no way to get the front sight hidden by one side of the rear sight. Simply "dot the i" to ensure sight alignment. This sight works equally well in daylight conditions, and the

Big Dot is much easier for those of us with aging eyes to pick up.

Like night sights, there are a number of laser sight manufacturers. There are Picatinny/Weaver rail mounted, trigger guard mounted, internal, and grip lasers available. Some can be purchased for less than a hundred bucks and others can cost hundreds of dollars. Laser sights are good both in day and low light conditions. Many shooters, however, believe them to be a substitute for marksmanship skills. Even with laser sights, one must know how to bring a weapon on target and press the trigger in a controlled manner in order to get accurate hits on target. My Glock 23 has an NcSTAR® Laser Sight installed on its rail system. It is a quick way to get on target. However, I must still remember proper trigger control.

As with the laser and night sites, there are numerous manufacturers of weapon mounted flashlights. These are advantageous because they illuminate the area that the weapon is pointing, which should be at the threat. Many laser rail systems can be used to integrate the weapon mounted flashlight system – thus providing both an aiming device with an illumination device. Again, caution should be heeded in that nothing is a substitute for proper trigger control!

Flashlight Techniques

If you are one of those who prefer a flashlight separate from your weapon, and there are many who do, then you need to be familiar with how to incorporate the flashlight into your weapons handling. There are a number of techniques that I will present. Try them all and determine which works best for you.

FBI Flashlight Technique

The first flashlight technique to gain popularity was developed by the Federal Bureau of Investigation – hence its name. This is a hands separated flashlight technique, meaning that the weapon hand and the flashlight hand are separated, requiring the shooter to fire one-handed. To perform a FBI flashlight technique, hold the flashlight in a sword or ice pick grip, depending on the flashlight's switch configuration. If your flashlight has a side slide switch, then hold in a sword grip with the thumb of your weak hand on the slide switch. If your flashlight has a side push button switch, then hold in an ice pick grip. If your flashlight has an end cap push button, hold it in an ice pick grip also.

Photo 2 – FBI Technique

Regardless of the grip, the flashlight should be held away from the body. Originally, it was taught being held high (above the head), away from the body and just forward of the body. The premise behind this was that an adversary would tend to fire at the flashlight beam; therefore by holding it away from the body, one was preventing center mass hits coming from the adversary. Considering that the human eye is drawn to light and movement, this makes good sense.

Variations of this technique are to bring the flashlight directly out to the side of your shoulder instead of above your head or low down by your leg. If you choose to use this technique and are engaged in a long search or shoot and move situation, varying the heights of the flashlight then becomes a guessing game for your adversary.

A disadvantage to this technique that was identified early on is the inaccuracy typical of a one-hand grip on the handgun.

Harries Flashlight Technique

In the early 1970s Michael Harries, a retired Marine, developed this flashlight technique. The technique is a hands together technique. It is performed by holding the flashlight in an ice pick grip with the switch on the finger side of the hand, versus the thumb side. Switch manipulation is accomplished by using the middle finger to push or slide the switch for large flashlights, or the thumb for end cap switched flashlights.

Photo 3 – Harries Technique

The weak hand holding the flashlight then is placed under the strong hand holding the pistol. The strong hand rests on top of the weak hand wrist and the weak hand is bent up to contact the back of the strong hand. This provides a very strong and stable shooting platform that ensures that where the weapon is pointed so is the flashlight. It works exceptionally well with the Weaver stance previously discussed. The Harries technique is probably the most used flashlight technique in use today, and one that I recommend.

Detractors argue that the technique only works with the Weaver stance and that the light beam is inline with the center of mass of the shooter. Many also are concerned that during recoil the light beam will momentarily be taken off of the attacker.

Rogers Surefire™ Flashlight Technique

With newer, smaller, end cap switched lights the Rogers Surefire™ flashlight technique was developed for use with the Surefire™ flashlights. This technique only works with smaller, end cap switched flashlights. To perform the technique, hold the flashlight between your index and middle finger like a syringe. Take a normal grip on the firearm and support with the weak hand. With a Surefire™ light that has the grip-ring equipped light, the end cap switch is held against the thumb pad and the light is activated by applying pressure to (e.g., pulling) the tail cap switch into the thumb pad.

Photo 4 – Rogers Surefire™ Technique

In this photo I am using a modified Rogers Surefire™ technique because I am using a Mini-Mag light with a tail cap switch. The Mini-Mag does not have the grip-ring common to the Surefire™ light. I activate the tail cap switch with the thumb tip of the strong hand, using the Isosceles stance.

I like and have used all three of these techniques. Each provides unique advantages and disadvantages. Even though I have used all three, I still prefer the Harries technique for non-mounted flashlight work.

Tactical Techniques

When faced with a self defense situation, both at home and away, there are a number of tactical techniques that one can benefit from understanding and employing. Many of these will be discussed in this section. Each concept can be used in many situations that are only limited by the practitioner's imagination.

Cover vs. Concealment

Many may have heard the terms cover and concealment, and many more probably understand the difference between these, but a refresher on these concepts is never outdated. What is the difference between cover and concealment? Simply stated, cover is anything that will stop incoming rounds from penetrating. As a defensive handgunner, one should seek cover when engaged, or about to engage, in a gun battle. Cover will save your life, if properly utilized!

Concealment is nothing more than an item that will conceal your presence or movement. Dry wall in a house will conceal your movement between rooms, but will not stop a round. A sheet separating two rooms will conceal you, but a round will eat right through it. Thin wood tables overturned will conceal you, but may not stop an incoming round.

Cover is substantial. A vehicle is cover. A cement wall is cover. A tree is cover. A heavy metal door is cover. If cover is not available, concealment is better than standing in the open exchanging fire but remember that concealment will not stop incoming rounds.

Fatal Funnel

This term is typically applied to a doorway. If you are on the inside of a room and someone is in your house, you will most likely be focused on the doorway because to get to you the invader will have to come through the door, which turns into a fatal funnel. This principle works in reverse. If you have an intruder in the house and you must move from your position to protect a family member, you too will encounter fatal funnels. Hallways, doorways, windows, aisles, or anything else that channels a person's movement are all considered fatal funnels.

Fatal Funnel

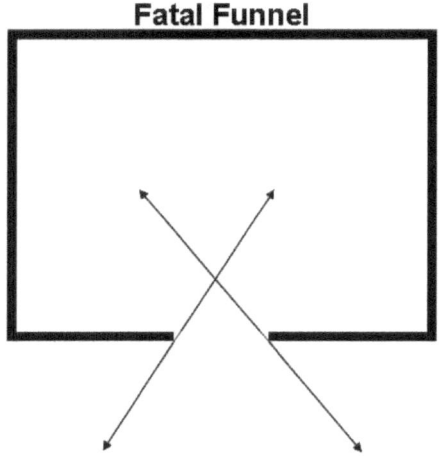

Figure 8 – Fatal Funnel

Tactically sound movement through fatal funnels requires speed. Which is more difficult to hit – a stationary or moving target? Of course a moving target is more difficult to hit. This then is how one minimizes the danger imposed by fatal funnels – move quickly through anything that channels your movement and quickly seek cover after getting through the funnel.

Quick Peek

A quick peek is a way of seeing around a corner or into a doorway while maintaining your position behind cover or concealment. One performs a quick peek by facing the wall of the corner or door that is about to be explored. While remaining behind cover/concealment, quickly move your head to the side looking around the corner or into the door and then immediately bring your head back behind cover/concealment. Do not expose more than one eye around the corner or door. This minimizes your exposure, while still allowing you to see.

If more than one quick peek is necessary to ensure the area is clear or to pinpoint the location of an adversary, then each subsequent quick peek should be performed at a different height. For instance, if your first quick peek was from head level, then the next quick peek should be at a level of your waist or knee. This will require you to perhaps go to a knee, which further reduces your vulnerability. The reason for varying the height each time a quick peek is performed from the same corner or door is to confuse a potential attacker so they cannot simply train their weapon on a spot and pull the trigger as soon as they see movement.

Quick peeks can be done with the gun in a ready position facing the corner or the doorway to be looked into. The way to do this is to back away from the corner or doorway to where the weapon can be brought to a low ready position. A low ready position is where your weapon is dropped down below your line of sight, but is still ready to be brought up and on target quickly.

Limited Penetration

Limited penetration is a way of engaging a target around a corner or through a doorway without completely rounding the corner or entering the doorway. The weapon should be brought up to a firing position and the defensive handgunner

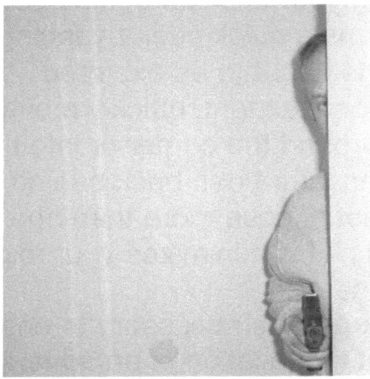

Photo 5 – Limited Penetration

simply leans out around the corner or into the doorway utilizing available cover and minimizing exposure while bringing the weapon to bear. Nothing more than the barrel of the weapon and one eye should protrude away from cover, as seen in this photograph. Once the position has been established, if there are no incoming rounds, the defensive handgunner can maintain this position indefinitely.

Cutting the Pie

Cutting the Pie (sometimes called the Angle of Incidence) is a very slow and deliberate technique. It is used when clearing around a corner, and it can also be used in clearing into a room through a doorway. It begins with the defensive handgunner facing the corner, while still near the wall. In a standing position with the muzzle of the weapon pointed toward the threat, make small, shuffling steps away from the wall. At the end of the shuffle step lean out very slowly. The weapon should be pointed just slightly inward toward the corner.

Cutting the Pie

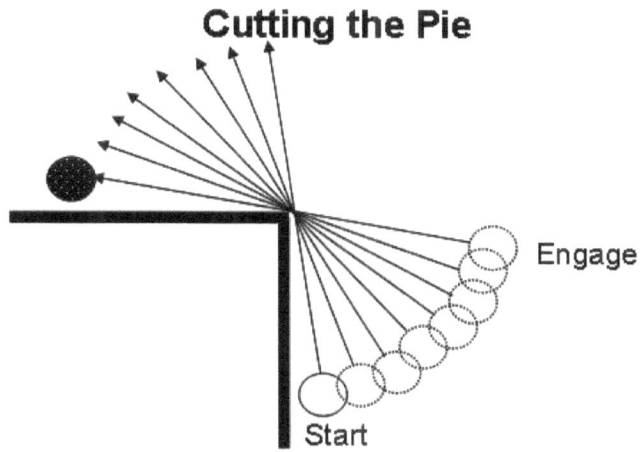

Figure 9 – Cutting the Pie

This allows looking outside the arm, while ensuring the shooting arm does not obstruct vision all the way to the floor or ground.

In this figure, the good guy is the series of blank circles on the right and the bad guy is the filled in circle on the left. Note how the slow shuffle step with lean out can allow recognition without exposing oneself. If done properly, the good guy will actually be able to see part of the bad guy without the bad guy seeing the good guy.

The slower this technique is conducted and the further away from the corner it is started, the better it will work. Using this technique will allow a glimpse of anyone around the corner. This glimpse may be of only a shoe, clothing, chest, or even a portion of head before the person sees you. This tactic allows the safe negotiation of corners in high danger situations where an aggressor may be lying in wait. Additionally, this pie technique can be used to partially clear a room without having to enter. The only spots that may not be seen inside a room using this technique are the absolute corners.

Remember, what can be seen can be shot. After identifying a threat, shots can be taken simply by making a slight lean out (roll over) to bring the weapon into play.

Seven Meter Side Step

Like many of these individual tactics, the Seven Meter Side Step was developed by the Israelis back in the 1960s and 1970s. Typically employed at the conclusion of Cutting the Pie when an adversary is identified, the Seven Meter Side Step is a way of moving into a firing position while maintaining the element of surprise. It is performed by stepping out as far to the side with the leg nearest the corner while leaning the foot and leg remaining behind cover and dropping into a crouched position.

Photo 6 – Seven Meter Side-Step

What this does is gets your center mass down and away from the corner. This is a good technique if the bad guy is focused on the corner awaiting your coming around it. It maintains the element of surprise by coming into the open and down and away from the corner. Your weapon should be in the firing position and ready to direct accurate fire as soon as the maneuver is complete with you in the low crouch position away from the corner. Quick recovery is possible since the trailing leg remains at the point of cover. By simply pushing off with the crouched leg, one is able to return to the safety of cover quickly.

Of course the downside to this technique is that one must leave cover in order to perform the technique. If you are unsure of your target or skeptical of your ability to hit the target, then this technique should not be used – substitute the Limited Penetration for this technique.

Door Entries

During a home invasion, a defensive handgunner may have the need to move from room to room either in search of the invader or to protect other family members. Should this become necessary then one must understand the safest means of entering rooms through doorways. There are two techniques presented – button hook and crisscross.

Door Entries

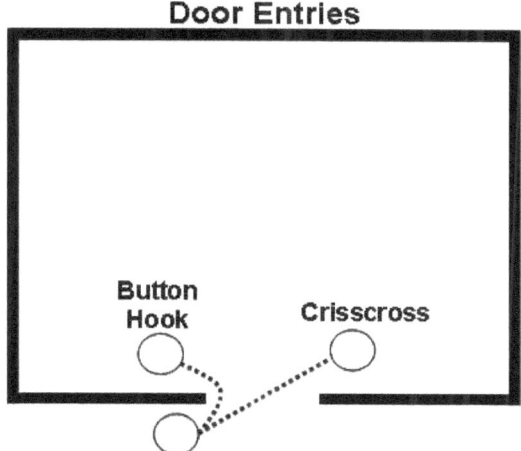

Figure 10 – Door Entries

The button hook is performed by facing the door about to be entered and quickly moving into the door threshold and hooking around the doorframe. A crisscross door entry is performed by facing the doorway about to be entered and moving quickly through the threshold to the other side of the doorway on the room interior. Both of these techniques are the best way to enter a doorway. Even with a crisscross, one is framed in the fatal funnel for a minimum amount of time.

After practice, one will determine the crisscross is the cuicker of the two techniques. Then why would someone want to perform a button hook? If it is known that the threat is in a corner that would be behind the person entering the doorway using a crisscross, then it would not be tactically sound to put ones back to the threat – thus the need for performing a button hook.

A theory that has been born out and used in actual operations that may be useful to know is that of the high right round. Consider that approximately 85% of the people in the world are right handed. Next time on the range observe right handed shooters. If they tend to reflexively fire their first round, note where the majority of these first rounds strike the target, which will be high and to the right. This is a simple result of jerking the trigger, which tends to throw the first round fired high and to the right. Understanding this theory and applying its logic, then one who must enter through a doorway not knowing where the threat is inside, would want to enter to the side of the doorway away from a high right round. This must be understood from the shooter's perspective on the inside. That is if a shooter is aiming at the doorway, is startled by someone entering, and jerks off a reflexive shot, then the errant round would strike to the right of the doorway looking from the inside. This would actually be to the person entering the room's left side, looking at the doorway. Consequently, one would want to enter moving from left to right, which in the case of the previous figure would require a crisscross entry.

One time the high right round theory should be discarded is when facing an unknown threat inside a room where the door opens inward, which most likely are all the doors in a home. In this case, one must enter to the hinge side of the door first to ensure no threat exists behind the door. A good technique for this is to use the weak hand to grasp the door knob, crouch below door knob level, turn the knob and swing the door inward while shouldering the door with the weak side. Drive the door to the wall. If there is resistance, perform a limited penetration on the door to determine the invader has not taken up position behind the door.

The most important aspect of entering doors is to do it quickly in order to exit the fatal funnel as fast as possible. Next in order of door entry priority is to clear the immediate threat. As one is moving through the doorway and an attacker presents themselves who has the opportunity and ability to cause great bodily harm or death, then feeling in jeopardy, take the shot and continue to move.

Corners are the most dangerous points of a room that has just been entered because if the immediate threat is being cleared during door entry, the corners are the areas that will be seen last, and in the case of a single person door entry, one corner will actually be behind the enterer. After clearing the immediate threat, clear to the corner on the side being entered and then quickly turn and visually clear to the opposite corner.

Once securely inside a room and corners have been cleared, if it is the intent to stay within the room, move to the most advantageous point of control. If cover is available, use it. If it is not available, use concealment. If neither cover nor concealment is available, move to a corner and control the room from there.

Shoot and Move

Enough cannot be said about the shoot and move technique. Do not present a stationary target for your adversary. Once engaged in a gun battle, triple tap and move either right or left. Simply moving a foot could save your life if return fire is incoming. This sideward movement can be combined with moving to the rear, or closer to your attacker if need be. Never stand still after firing your triple tap unless securely behind significant cover.

<u>Home Defense</u>

Your family should have a self defense plan, just as I would hope you have a fire escape plan. Each member of the family should know their responsibility in the event of a home invasion. Someone should be assigned to call 911, and someone else responsible for confirming the presence of all family members. Rendezvous points both inside and outside the house should be identified and taught to all family members.

Such defense plans must be based on personal circumstances. These circumstances involve the type of house one has – is it a single or multi-story home, detached home or a small apartment? If a detached home, does it have a split floor plan where some members of the family are located on one side and others on the other side of the home? Answers to these questions will determine what the defense plan will be.

In a multi-story house with all family members sleeping on the upper floors if an invader breaks in on the bottom floor, the ideal plan would be to simply defend from the top of the stairway while all other family members congregate in one room with one person assigned to call the police. An invader breaks in to a single story consolidated floor plan home with just a couple sharing the same bedroom, the best defense plan would be for both people to take cover behind the bed, one covers the door with the defensive handgun, and the other calls the police. In a family occupied consolidated floor plan home, the plan should be for the adults to assemble in the youngest child's room with the other children being shepparded into that one room. All family members take cover behind the bed, the armed defender covers the door, and another calls the police.

The single family split floor plan family occupied home presents the most danger to the defenders. In this case the two adults should have access to arms. One remains in the spouse's bedroom behind cover, covers the door, and calls police. The other, using tactical movement techniques, moves to the other side of the home, consolidates the other family members in one room, all take cover behind the bed, the defender covers the door, and all wait of the police to arrive. Should either of the two armed defenders decide to link back up with the other one, a verbal code should be developed to communicate who is about to come through a door. Since both should be in defensive positions ready to bring the intruder under fire should the intruder enter, it would be tragic that a family member enter and the defender accidentally shoot the family member. Develop a verbal code system and let all family members know the code.

These examples point out two very important concepts. The first is that this is true home defense. Defenders do not need to go looking for an intruder. Let the intruder come to you and use the fatal funnel concept to the invader's disadvantage. Secondly, is notifying the police. It is important to get police enroute as soon as possible. If the intruder leaves, then police can more quickly locate the intruder. If the intruder remains in the house, police can clear the house. If the intruder has been engaged by the defender, the police will be needed to get any medical assistance necessary and to document the nature of the self defense use of deadly force. Defend the home and call the police!

Another scenario that may be encountered by the home defender is an intruder or thief breaking in to vehicles or out buildings. In this case, the homeowner should call the police. While you have the legal right to protect your property from thieves, it is not tactically sound to leave your home in pursuit of or to prevent the loss of property. With this said, I realize this may be a hard pill to swallow for some, but recognize that your life and the lives of your loved ones are more important than anything you may own. For this reason my recommendation is to protect the home and family and let the insurance company replace any lost property.

There are many security products on the market that can help in the defense of property. Think lighting, landscaping, locks, and alarms. Have the local law enforcement agency come out and conduct a home security assessment for recommendations on these types of products.

Outside Home Defense

Robbery and aggravated assault constitute the vast majority (92%) of reported violent crime. Attempts to commit these crimes will most likely occur outside of the home, while walking to your car or a restaurant or any number of other places. A robbery may take the form of someone snatching a woman's purse and running, or could involve someone sticking a weapon in your back or face and demanding money.

Aggravated assault rarely occurs without some forewarning. Either the attacker has verbalized his intent to attack or made an overt move to attack.

Avoidance is the first defense against these types of attacks. Be aware of your surroundings and the people in the surroundings. Avoid bad parts of town, walk in well lit areas, travel in groups, and walk on the outside of the sidewalk to prevent someone from jumping you as you pass an alley entrance. There are numerous ways to avoid becoming a victim. This book does not cover avoidance, but rather focuses on when an encounter has begun.

Assuming situational awareness, forewarning will occur in both robbery and aggravated assault encounters. In these cases, basic defensive techniques can be employed to counter these crimes in your self defense. One defensive maneuver is performed by simply moving off the axis of attack.

In this graphic the attack is a frontal attack where the attacker is moving at you from your front.

Axis of Attack

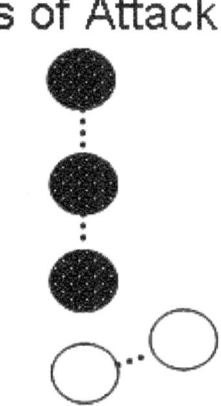

Figure 11 – Front Axis of Attack

A simple defense against this attack is to move off the axis of attack, use your weak hand to ward off an attacker, draw your handgun, and fire at your attacker. Combined with a crouch this is a very effective counter to this type of attack. Movement off the axis of attack, in the case of frontal assault, should be to your weapon side, which facilitates the use of your weak arm to fend off the attack and allow for drawing your weapon.

Creating distance is another concept that can be used to buy time for bringing your weapon to bear against an attacker. Using the same frontal assault scenario, one could simply back pedal away from your attacker while drawing your weapon. Again, the movement should be off the axis of attack and should be made to your weapon side. Once the weapon is in your hand, you are ready to stand your ground and protect yourself.

Suppose your attacker is already in your face and there is no opportunity to move sideways or create distance. It is now or never! Use your weak hand palm to deliver an upward blow to the bottom of the nose or perform an eye rake, while at the same time drawing your weapon and firing into your attacker.

Frontal assaults are much easier to defend because you most likely will see them coming. Rear assaults are more difficult and present the greatest danger, and will require calm steady nerves, wit, diversion and distraction.

Rear Assault

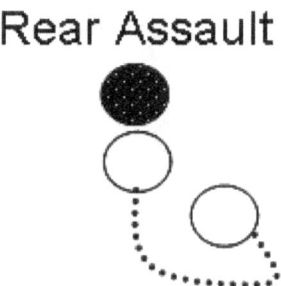

Figure 12 – Rear Assault

Consider a scenario where an armed robber comes up behind you, sticks a hard object that you presume is a weapon of some sort in your back, and demands your money. The robber could be armed with a firearm themselves, so this is a very dangerous situation. Before making any movement, start talking to your would be robber. Tell him you will give him all you have, but please don't kill you. Begin to reach to your rear pocket as though you are going for your wallet while talking to the robber. The object is to keep your assailant listening and talking.

As the conversation is going on, begin to turn around because it is natural for two people who are talking to one another to be facing each other. While turning, assess your assailant in an effort to determine what type of weapon they have, and if possible move slightly away from your attacker. Continue to talk to the attacker. Say anything that comes to mind. Ask him why he is robbing you. Engaging him in conversation is the diversion/distraction.

My experience and study shows that it is difficult for someone to do two things at once, like talk and pull a trigger at the same time. While the robber is talking, they are distracted from their intention of robbing you, and perhaps of killing you. This buys time for you to assess the situation. While this verbal exchange is ongoing, you have turned to face your attacker and created a small distance while appearing as though you are reaching for your wallet. At this point you must make a decision – do I give him my wallet or do I draw and fire? You are the only one who can make this decision, but this is a technique to buy time for you to make the decision. The most important thing is to engage in conversation and try to get the assailant to talk.

Inside Vehicle Defense

Self defense encounters may occur while ether in or around vehicles. We have all heard of road rage and carjacking incidents. While there are techniques for firing out of moving vehicles, these go beyond the scope of this book. Incidents of road rage should not be dealt with in a self defense manner while vehicles are moving. Of course no rule is cemented in stone – it is difficult enough to either drive or fire without the distraction of the other. Consequently, if someone is exhibiting road rage by attempting to wreck you or run you off the road, then firing while driving may be required. If faced with this situation, realize that if the two vehicles are side-by-side at roughly the same speed, no unique technique for hitting your target is required. The speed of the bullet is faster than the cars going side-by-side so no lead need be taken into account. My personal recommendation though, is if faced with this type of idiot on the road, simply slow down and pull off the road. Let them go on their way. Only if the enraged driver stops and begins to approach is the need for self defense necessary.

Carjacking is another issue altogether. These most often happen as the victim is getting into the car or has stopped for whatever reason, such as a traffic control device (i.e., red light, stop sign, etc.). In the event someone approaches as you are getting into the vehicle your situational awareness should have identified the potential threat and techniques discussed in the previous section can be used.

Physical security measures can often prevent carjacking when the vehicle is stopped. Keep doors locked and windows rolled up. If the carjacker cannot get in the vehicle, they most likely will be unsuccessful. However, there are times that armed carjackers approach the vehicle while it is stopped and threaten the victim into giving up the car. Simply flooring the accelerator and driving away should prevent these types of carjackings. If unable to escape, then self defense is the final option.

Here are some facts on cars and handguns that take on mythical proportion in Hollywood films. Cars can and do stop handgun ammunition. When fired into a car door, a handgun round does not penetrate into the passenger compartment a majority of the time. If the window happens to be down, then the minor possibility of a handgun round penetrating a door is minimized further.

Handgun rounds will penetrate automotive glass, creating glass fragments along with the projectile. Therefore, to protect yourself from an incoming round through a window, slump into the seat bringing the vehicle body metal into play for cover.

Handgun rounds will flatten tires. While this is entirely probable, they do not cause blowouts like seen in the movies. I recall a car chase that I was involved in where another officer unloaded his service revolver into the back tires of an eluding pickup truck. He successfully hit the tires, but they did not go flat immediately. In fact, he had time to retrieve the shotgun and fire all five rounds from it at the tires without penetration of the buck shot. The tires did leak down slowly and finally became a factor in stopping this criminal, but happened in a much less dramatic fashion than one is led to believe by Hollywood.

The engine block provides the most cover on a vehicle. This is entirely true and should be used to your advantage if ever involved in a shootout around vehicles.

I have discussed these facts and myths for a reason, and that is to impress upon the reader that vehicles make very good cover from both the inside and the outside. Use this to your advantage. Recognize it and if possible turn the table on the carjacker.

Defensive handguns, in order to be useful, must be reachable. Know your state's law on handguns in vehicles. Some states require they be in plain site, others require they be concealed, and all that have concealed weapons laws make it legal for concealed weapons permit holders to have the weapons concealed in the passenger compartment. Be prepared to draw and use the weapon when faced with a carjacking, if unable to exit the scene.

Realizing the fact that vehicles provide great cover, this can work to your advantage in another way. If involved in a shootout where the attacker takes cover behind a vehicle but does not place themselves behind the tires to stop incoming rounds, be aware that you can ricochet rounds under the car and into the legs of the attacker. Ricochet rounds are surprisingly accurate when fired at less than a forty-five degree angle to a concrete surface (this works for block walls as well).

Simply aim your sights at a forty-five degree or less angle to the hard surface in line with the attacker's legs. Squeeze off the round and it will strike the hard surface, ricochet and travel under the vehicle and hit the attacker in the legs. This should end the encounter.

I have actually seen this ricochet technique work on indoor drywall when fired at a shallow enough angle. Keep this technique in mind when engaged inside buildings if you cannot get a clear shot on an attacker hidden behind partial cover.

Reloading and Dealing with Malfunctions

With regard to ensuring one has ammunition in the weapon; there are two situations that can determine the safe outcome of an extended gun battle. These situations include knowing how and when to reload a weapon and how to clear any malfunctions that may occur while engaged in the gun battle.

Reloading

Every defensive handgunner needs to practice reloading skills and develop proficiency in reloading in order to ensure that it can be done without thinking during the heat of battle. Reloading skills should be honed to the point of being able to reload without looking at the weapon. It should become second nature. Considering that most encounters will occur in low light conditions, developing one's reloading skills to this point are a necessity.

Regardless of whether one carries a revolver or a semi-automatic handgun. There are only two types of reloads to be concerned with – emergency and tactical.

Emergency Reload

An emergency reload occurs when the weapon has ran out of ammunition and must be replenished to continue the battle until victorious. Running out of ammunition with a high-capacity semi-automatic is not that difficult to do. With high-capacity semi-automatics, a gun battle should be over with by the time the need to reload occurs. However, reality proves this may not always be the case, so owners of these weapons need to practice emergency reloading as much as a revolver shooter does.

Revolvers, since they have a limited number of rounds (normally five or six), one would think an emergency reload should never occur – that the shooter should be counting rounds and never have an emergency reload. While this is what defensive handgunners who carry a revolver should strive for and it may work on the range, many things happen during a gun battle and the ability to concentrate on how many rounds have been fired may be difficult to remember. Therefore, both the revolver and semi-automatic handgunner should practice reloading.

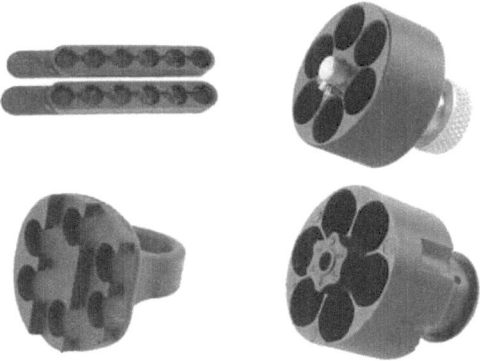

Photo 7 – Assorted Revolver Speedloaders

This photo depicts various types of revolver speedloaders that are on the market. Bianchi Speed Strips™ are shown in the top left. These are simple rubber strips designed to hold .38 or .357 bullets. To employ the Speed Strips either one or two rounds are inserted into the cylinder at a time, and the speed strip pulled away from the bullets, allowing the bullets to settle into the cylinder.

In the top right photo is the HKS Speedloader. Like the Maxfire and Safariland, it is designed to hold six rounds of ammunition. To employ the HKS speedloader all six rounds are inserted into the cylinder and the locking knob is turned, releasing the six rounds. The Maxfire speedloader (bottom left) is similar to the Bianchi Speed Strips™ in that it is made of rubber and the speedloader is simply ripped away from the bullets. Safariland's design (bottom right) has a push in release; whereas, the shooter inserts all six rounds into the cylinder and pushes against the round extractor, which releases the rounds into the cylinder.

Reloading revolvers is quick. It can be done with the speedloaders described here in about six seconds. The most important part of quickly reloading a revolver, though, requires several steps. In the first step, the shooter opens the cylinder. The cylinder release will be functioned using the thumb of the right hand and the cylinder is pushed through the frame with the ring and middle fingers of the left hand. While this occurs, the right hand should be reaching for the speedloader. The thumb of the left hand, which is now holding the revolver, should be placed on the extractor rod, while turning the revolver muzzle up. Gravity is the key to successfully reloading a revolver in a fast manner. The left thumb pushes the extractor rod, with the muzzle pointed straight up, dumping the spent brass on the ground. The loaded speedloader is in the right hand beginning movement to the cylinder of the revolver. The left hand is now turning the revolver so its muzzle is pointed down at the ground. The two hands come together with the right hand maneuvering the rounds into the cylinder. Be sure all six rounds are inserted. Then, depending on which of the above speedloader you have, the knob is turned, the speedloader is ripped from the bullets, or the speedloader is pushed in hard against the cylinder extractor, all of which release the bullets into the cylinder. The left hand closes the cylinder, rotates it until it locks, and the weapon is brought back into play. These actions can be done in much less time than it took to read this description of how to perform an emergency reload of a revolver.

To conduct an emergency reload of a semi-automatic pistol, realize that the slide will lock back on an empty magazine. The weapon is designed to function this way. Once the slide has locked to the rear, the shooter should depress the magazine release button with the shooting hand. Ensure the magazine well is facing down. Again, use gravity to assist in reloading.

As the magazine release is being activated, the shooter should be reaching for a full magazine with the non-shooting hand. Grasp the magazine, and while continuing to hold the weapon in the direction of the threat, move the full magazine to the magazine well. Insert the full magazine into the magazine well and slide it home. Tap the base of the magazine to ensure it is seated and release the slide lock. The weapon is now fully reloaded and ready to engage the attacker, if needed.

Tactical Reload

This is the second type of reload that defensive handgunners need to perfect. A tactical reload occurs when there is a lull in the gun battle, or rounds have been fired and you are now behind cover and want to reload. The purpose of a tactical reload is to reload the weapon to its full capacity. In the previous explanation of emergency reloading, speedloaders and magazines where simply dumped without regard for retrieving or maintaining them. With a tactical reload, it may be wise to retain the non-expended rounds just in case they may be needed later.

A tactical reload of a revolver is where the Bianchi Speed Strips™ excels. One can dump only one or two rounds from a revolver and replenish with only what is needed. Otherwise all rounds would need to be dropped and the cylinder reloaded completely. This technique should only be attempted when behind substantial cover because it may take longer than six seconds to perform. If a revolver tactical reload is being done without substantial cover, then conduct a total reload as though it is an emergency reload. Better to leave live rounds on the ground and get a full cylinder to work with than to wind up dead with one or two empty rounds in your hand.

Tactically reloading a semi-automatic can be done anywhere and at anytime during an encounter. The shooter needs to anticipate when a tactical reload may occur in order to prepare for the quickest possible reload. While the weapon is still pointed toward the threat, the weak hand reaches for a fully loaded magazine. Once retrieved, the magazine is moved up alongside the weapon grip. At a time dictated by the shooter, the magazine release is depressed and the magazine falls out. The full magazine is then inserted into the magazine well and firmly tapped in to ensure positive seating of the magazine has occurred. Since the slide did not lock to the rear, there is no need to rack the slide to load a round.

Most semi-automatic handguns manufactured today are capable of firing without a magazine inserted. Of course one must be absolutely certain the weapon will fire without a magazine inserted. There are some semi-automatic pistols available that have a magazine safety, which does not allow it to be fired without the magazine locked in place. Know your gun!

Weapon Malfunctions

Weapon malfunctions seldom happen, but one must prepare for the unexpected. If faced with a malfunction during a self defense encounter, you should be able to respond instinctively instead of dying for failure to prepare. There are basically three types of malfunctions that can happen with only two of them occurring in revolvers. They are failure to fire, failure to eject, and double feed. These are also known as Type I, II and III malfunctions, respectively.

Type I (Failure to Fire)

As the name implies, this is where the trigger is pressed and the gun does not go bang as expected. There are a number of possible causes of this – a round is not under the hammer, bad primer, sunken primer, or there is a weak hammer spring.

Clearing this type failure in a revolver is accomplished simply by pulling the trigger again – thus rotating a fresh round under the hammer. If a revolver is experiencing this failure on a regular basis, the spring tension needs to be tightened. All defensive revolvers equipped with an adjustable main spring should have the main spring tightened as much as it will go without overly exerting foot pounds of energy with a screwdriver.

Failure to fire in a semi-automatic handgun requires more effort to clear and get the weapon back into firing condition. A simple three-step process clears this malfunction. This process is known as tap-rack-fire. One of the reasons a round may not be chambered is that the magazine was not fully seated into the weapon. Understanding this truism, the first step is tap; whereby, the shooter taps the bottom of the magazine in an effort to fully seat the magazine. Next, the shooter racks the slide back and slightly tilts the handgun to the right, which ejects a round that may have had a bad primer, and releases the slide to pick up and chamber the next round out of the magazine. DO NOT RIDE THE SLIDE. That is, do not hold the slide and ride it in, rather release the slide and let the spring do its job. At this point the shooter has the weapon back in service and is able to reengage, or fire the weapon.

To practice this technique using a revolver simply load only five rounds into a six round cylinder and place the empty chamber in the appropriate pre-stage cylinder spot. For example, Smith and Wesson revolver cylinders rotate counter-clockwise, looking at the cylinder from the rear. Consequently, the pre-stage cylinder position would be immediately to the right of the cylinder under the hammer. When the trigger is pulled in the double-action mode, the hammer will fall on the rotated empty cylinder – thus giving the sense of a failure to fire situation. Practice the technique of pulling the trigger again to rotate a live round under the hammer. As you will see, this takes no time to get the weapon back in action.

Semi-automatic shooters can also practice this technique. Remove the magazine from the weapon, pull the slide to the rear ejecting whatever round is in the chamber, release the slide and let it slam closed, and then replace the magazine into the magazine well and ram it home. The weapon now has its firing pin engaged to fire, but without a round in the chamber, one will simply get a snap as the trigger is pulled and the firing pin is released. At this point, practice the tap, rack and fire technique previously discussed.

CAUTION: Conduct these practice sessions with live ammunition and only at a firing range. Remember the "all guns are always loaded" rule!

Type II (Failure to Eject)

This failure is most often encountered in the semi-automatic pistol. It occurs when a fired round does not fully extract before the slide goes forward. Another name for this malfunction is the "stove pipe" jam. Failure to eject can prevent a new round from being chambered. Older, short ejector, semi-automatics tend to be afflicted with this failure more so than newer semi-automatic handguns. To clear this failure, follow the tap, rack and fire method previously discussed for failure to fire malfunctions.

While the semi-automatic handgun typically is the weapon associated with this malfunction, I have seen revolvers that fail to eject a spent round also. Most of these I have seen are a result of handloaded ammunition that was either reloaded too many times, which wears the rim down on the shell casing, or contained too much powder creating too high of pressures in the cylinder.

Semi-automatic handgunners can also practice this malfunction by manually setting up the failure to eject. If practicing at home in a dry fire environment, simply open the slide, lock it back, insert a round of spent brass into the chamber in a standing up (e.g., stovepipe) manner, and release the slide lock onto the empty round of brass. Now insert the magazine. Point the weapon in a safe direction and pull the trigger. The firing pin is engaged when the slide was released and the pulling of the trigger will drop the firing pin without any effect. Then simply complete the tap, rack, and fire drill mentioned before.

First step in preventing this malfunction in a revolver is to keep it from happening in the first place. Never carry reloaded ammunition as your carry ammo. Reloads are fine for practice, but rely only on quality manufactured ammunition for all your self-defense needs. The prior list in this book provides recommendations on ammunition.

Should this situation happen during a self defense encounter, the most prudent solution is to use a backup weapon, if one is available. Barring that, create as much distance as possible and seek cover. This revolver malfunction is not one that will be cleared quickly. If the extractor leaves a round in the cylinder, most likely the extractor will not seat itself with new ammo, rendering the weapon inoperative. If hot ammunition caused the failure to eject, most likely it will not be possible to push the extractor rod hard enough to get the round unseated from within the cylinder. In either case, the round will have to be forcibly removed. Refer to the first step to prevent this from happening in the first place.

Type III (Double Feed)

A Type III Double Feed malfunction is seen only in semi-auto pistols and does not occur in revolvers. Implied by the name is that two rounds are trying to basically occupy the same space at the same time. Most often this is set-up by a failure to eject whereby the extractor does not pull the fired round out of the chamber, but the slide still moves to the rear and attempts to load another round into the chamber. This is an obvious visually observable malfunction because the slide does not go all the way forward and there will be brass easily seen jammed into the rear of the brass that occupies the chamber.

Clearing a double feed malfunction is more time consuming than the previous two malfunctions discussed. To clear this malfunction one must lock, strip the magazine, rack, rack, rack; reinsert a fresh magazine; rack and fire. First lock the slide to the rear. Then depress the magazine release. If it is a true Type III malfunction the magazine most likely will not simply fall from the magazine well – thus it must be striped out of the magazine well by gripping the base of the magazine and physically pulling it out of the pistol. Throw this magazine to the ground in case it was the cause of the double feed.

Once the magazine is out of the pistol, grasp the slide, pull it to the rear and release it to ram forward, rack the slide again to eject the round in the chamber, and once more rack the slide to ensure the round is ejected. At this point, insert a new magazine, rack the slide again, and the weapon is ready to fire.

On double feed malfunctions remember to lock the slide, strip the magazine and discard it, rack the slide three times, insert a new magazine, rack the slide to load a fresh round, and then be ready to fire.

Again, this malfunction can be staged by locking the slide to the rear, inserting a spent casing into the chamber by hand, inserting a magazine, hold a second spent casing in the breach and slowly releasing the slide onto the spent case in the breach. Now there are two cases trying to load (e.g., the double feed). Now point the weapon in a safe direction and practice the clearing process.

Many tactics and techniques for the defensive handgunner have been presented in this chapter. Reading and understanding these is only half the battle. One must practice these techniques regularly to ensure they become second nature when faced with a self defense situation. I remember what an old colleague of mine once said, "Your adversary practices and if you are not practicing, then when the two of you meet, you will lose." Do not become a victim from lack of preparation!

Chapter 7

Mentally Preparing
for a
Lethal Confrontation

Victory at all costs, victory in spite of all terror, victory however long and hard the road may be; for without victory, there is no survival.

Winston Churchill

My defensive tactics instructor in the police academy had a saying that when engaged in a life and death battle, "do whatever it takes to win. If this means kicking, hitting, biting, head butting, it doesn't matter. Do whatever it takes to go home at the end of the shift." This attitude probably saved my life in 1981.

I was working day shift on September 23, 1981 assigned to District 2. Another one-officer unit was dispatched to handle a domestic disturbance call and I was sent as backup. The call was in a government housing project where crime, violence and drugs were rampant and it was not unusual for officers in my department to be involved in domestic calls to this particular complex.

The primary officer arrived first. When I arrived the first officer had already placed his hands on the suspect and was trying to turn him toward the wall for handcuffing. My partner gave me the hurry up signal and I ran to the altercation. After seeing me, the suspect became violent and started to fight. Using a take down, I took the suspect to the ground where we all three continued to scuffle. Suddenly, I could see underneath the suspect and saw a revolver lying on the ground. I reached for it at the same time the suspect did. He got to it before me and a shot rang out. My partner grunted and fell back. He was hit.

The suspect rose up on a knee and pointed the gun at my partner as he was getting up off the ground. I grabbed the suspect's gun hand and began to pull it up. A second shot rang out. I could barely see my partner, but he fell backwards, as though he had received a second round center mass. In my mind, my partner was dead.

I continued to stay in contact with the suspect while maintaining a death grip on the cylinder of the revolver. A revolver cannot be fired double action if the cylinder cannot rotate a fresh chamber under the hammer and I had been trained on this. While I was able to prevent another round from going off, I needed to get the gun away from the suspect. We were both back on the ground at this point. I had control of the revolver's cylinder and was working to extract the suspect's trigger finger from the trigger guard.

Finally getting his finger out of the trigger guard, I bit down on the first joint of his trigger finger, almost removing this joint. This allowed me to get the revolver out of his hand, at which time I slid it away from us so it would no longer present a threat to me. Continuing to try to control the suspect, I noticed a shadow looming over me. I knew I was a goner, thinking one of the suspect's friends had come to help him. I looked over my shoulder and to my wondrous surprise it was my partner coming back to the fight. He was not dead. We were finally able to control the suspect and get the handcuffs on him. Backup and aid was called for over the radio, and in a matter of minutes the cavalry had arrived.

When the first round discharged it struck the cement walkway we were wrestling on. The bullet fragmented and entered my partner's thigh without striking bone or any major blood vessels. I prevented the second round from hitting my partner by pulling the suspect's arm away as the round was discharged.

After the second round was fired, my partner got back up, drew his weapon, but could not fire for fear of hitting me while I was still engaged with the suspect. My partner and I were transported to the hospital. I had received powder burns and various cuts and bruises, and he received bullet fragments to his leg. Both of us were released the same day.

The suspect was treated and released later that night from the injuries he sustained. He was charged with Aggravated Assault, went to trial, and eventually pled guilty before the case was given to the jury.

During this confrontation, I remembered what my defensive tactics instructor said about "whatever it takes." That is what I did, and I did go home after that shift. It is this mindset that must be ingrained before being involved in a deadly altercation.

In this chapter I will discuss mentally preparing yourself for that deadly altercation that I hope you are never faced with, but if you are, that you have mentally prepared yourself for it and that this book in someway helps.

Physical Reactions to Deadly Encounters

Since I published my first article on the physical responses to stress and need for stress induced firearms training in 1987, there has been an entire body of research conducted on what happens in the body during deadly force encounters. Obviously, most of this research has been conducted on law enforcement officers, which represents the largest body of personnel involved in deadly shootouts. Suffice it to say, that the following physiological reactions to a deadly force encounter are well documented.

Humans have evolved over time, but one of the most primitive instincts remaining is one of self-preservation. During the high stress involved in deadly force encounters, this instinct still comes out in human beings. Simply put, it is the "fight or flight" syndrome that most people have heard about. What does it mean from a physical perspective?

When faced with a deadly force encounter the body goes through a number of preparatory steps. These steps begin with a release of stress hormones such as adrenaline and cortisol. Once these hormones are released into the blood system, they result in a number of physical effects such as increased heart rate, blood pressure, and blood flow to large muscle groups, which prepare the body to fight or flee.

Respirations increase to ensure oxygenated blood flow to the parts of the body needed for strength or speed. Eye pupils dilate, which in turn has a negative effect on sight such as the loss of near vision, deceptive depth perception, and tunnel vision. Sweating becomes more profuse, while the mouth dries out. A less noticeable effect is slowed digestion because the body is sending blood away from organs not involved in fight or flight.

While these responses will enhance strength and gross motor skills from the major muscle groups, they will be detrimental to fine motor skills such as eye/hand coordination. With a reduction in fine motor skills, it becomes more difficult to fire a weapon accurately.

Degradation of the eye during high stress incidents like a deadly encounter is most concerning. In 1915, Dr. Walter Cannon determined that pupils of the eyes dilate, which leads to near vision degradation, during high stress incidents. Dr. Hal Breedlove has theorized that tunnel vision will reduce peripheral vision by as much as 70%, thus leaving a person with a tunnel of about 24 inches. Imagine what this can do for identifying the threat presented during a deadly encounter.

Another physical effect is auditory exclusion. Normally, the human body relies on its five senses to assess any given situation. When faced with a life or death event, the body tends to rely more heavily on the sense that can provide the most pertinent information possible, which turns out to be the sense of sight, at the exclusion of the other senses.

Consequently, parties involved in a deadly force encounter will suffer this effect and may very well give varying accounts of the facts of the incident. My incident, shared at the beginning of this chapter, is a prime example of auditory exclusion. Following the incident, my partner and I discussed the incident at length. We both knew that shots had been fired, but both of us gave a different number of rounds fired from what actually happened. I have already explained there were two shots fired, but when interviewed about this, my partner had counted six rounds and I had counted three rounds as being fired. This difference is a direct result of the auditory exclusion that we both suffered during that event.

These physical reactions are normal and expected during high stress incidents. There is no way to prevent them from occurring due to the evolutionary process and the instilled fight or flight response that all human beings have. However, there are ways to minimize these effects during a self defense deadly force situation.

Mind-Body Relationship

Before beginning to mentally prepare for a deadly force encounter, one must have an understanding of and appreciation for the fact that the mind and body work in conjunction. The mind-body relationship is important to understand because daily stressors play a part in our ability to handle the increased stress induced by a deadly force encounter.

Unfortunately, our bodies cannot differentiate between good and bad stress. The body's stress responses, as previously described, occur regardless of whether the stress is caused by physical or emotional events. Stress is cumulative. That is, our daily stress builds up and when faced with a deadly force situation, our stress may be unmanageable.

In 1967 Doctors Thomas Holmes and Richard Rahe conducted a study into stressful events, which ultimately led to the publication of the Holmes and Rahe Stress Scale. This research and stress scale development proves the body cannot differentiate good and bad stress. The following are examples of events and the stress rating associated for both good and bad events:

Life event	Stress
Death of a spouse	100
Divorce	73
Marriage	50
Retirement	45
Marital reconciliation	45
Pregnancy	40
Gain a new family member	39
Outstanding personal achievement	28
Vacation	13
Christmas	12

Figure 13 – Holmes and Rahe Stress Scale

While this list is representative of life events, it is not all inclusive of the research conducted. The point is that one can see that both good (marriage) and bad (divorce) events have stress associated with them. These are everyday types of events that have a physical effect. Combine these stressors with a deadly force encounter and one can see how it could cause overload – thus having a negative effect on how one reacts to the dangers of the event.

Fortunately, we can control our everyday stresses and prepare ourselves for the physical effects of a deadly force encounter.

Mental Preparation

Mentally preparing for a deadly force encounter involves relaxation techniques, visualization, and positive self-talk. Each of these will be discussed in the following sections. However, these alone will not provide the total tactical mindset that is needed to identify and survive a deadly encounter. A color code for tactical awareness will also be provided.

Relaxation Techniques

One of the most effective relaxation techniques is deep breathing (or combat breathing). Combine this with muscular relaxation and imagery and one can easily reduce the stressors of everyday life.

These relaxation techniques should be performed in a quiet, secluded area in order to maximize results. I prefer to lie on my back on the floor and place my hands on my lower abdomen. Martial artists will relate to this "Ki" technique of using our internal energy for relaxation. Eyes should be closed.

Deep breathing is a four step process, which includes:

1. Inhalation
2. Pause
3. Exhalation
4. Pause

Each step should be conducted for four seconds, so inhale deeply through the nostrils for four seconds. Then pause for four seconds, and exhale for four seconds. Exhalation should be through the mouth, and then pause for four seconds before repeating the four step process.

Concentrate on the deep inhalation, pause, exhalation and pause. Count in your head 1001, 1002, 1003, 1004 to ensure four seconds is devoted to each step in the process. By focusing on this breathing technique, one's mind is allowed to forget about the everyday stressors, which will ultimately allow total relaxation. The more this breathing technique is practiced, the quicker it takes effect in subsequent sessions.

As you begin to feel yourself relaxing through deep breathing, then is the time to incorporate the muscular relaxation technique. With this technique, focus on one spot of the body like your back. While continuing the deep breathing, tense your back muscles and hold them tense as you exhale for the four counts. Release the self-imposed muscle tensioning when the pause step begins after exhalation. Feel the tension flow away. Move to your legs and tense them during the next exhalation and release at the pause. Then move to your hands, ball your fists tight, hold for the four count exhalation and release. Finish with the feet – tense your toes, hold for the four count, and then release them. Feel all the tension leave your body as you continue the deep breathing process.

Next comes the imagery phase of relaxation. This is where you go to your favorite spot. You may love a mountain cabin sitting next to a mountain stream, or lying on the warm sand at the beach listening to the surf come ashore. Whatever you find peaceful and relaxing is the image you should conjure up in your mind. Imagine all the details, the warm sand, a slight ocean breeze, the salt smell, the surf crashing ashore, and the hot sun beating down. As with this last sentence, try to involve all of the senses. The more real your imagery is, the more relaxing it will be.

These relaxation techniques should be done for 20 minutes, which is a sufficient amount of time to totally relax. The importance of practicing this is that when faced with a deadly encounter, simply cycling through this deep breathing (combat breathing) routine will calm the nerves because you have conditioned your mind and body to relax through deep breathing.

Visualization

A number of stories have been written about visualization helping improve performance. One such story is about an American Prisoner of War (POW) kept in captivity in Vietnam for a number of years. The story goes that one technique he had for dealing with the isolation and other depravity he had to deal with was by mentally playing 18 holes of golf on his favorite golf course back home each day. After his release from years of captivity, he returned home and played the golf course he had been mentally playing for years. Without any practice, he went out and shot the best score of his life.

Another such story has a group of athletes who were divided into three groups. One group did nothing but physical practice in their sport, the second group did no practice, and the third group only did mental practice. At the conclusion of the test, the three groups were pitted against one another in one aspect of their sport. The results were that group one who had done only physical practice showed a marked improvement, group two who had done no practice showed no improvement, and group three who had done only mental practice showed an improvement similar to group one.

The point from all these stories is that visualization techniques work. Granted, there are skeptics of visualization techniques. However, consider these facts:

- Elite athletes and coaches use visualization techniques regularly. If it did not work, why would they waste their time?
- There are case studies that prove visualization tailored to individual needs has shown marked improvement in individual performance.
- Many scientific studies have been conducted that prove beyond doubt that visualization improves performance.

If another example of the success of visualization is needed for any of the skeptics out there, consider an article in the 2008 Golf Digest about Tiger Woods (the best golfer in the world today). Tiger's caddie was quoted saying, "…instead of spending hours on the practice field, he just tried to picture how he wanted to swing the club...." Tiger, himself, said in the same article that, "It's weird that it happens so quickly now. If we went through the whole process on one hole, it would sound really complicated. But now, I just understand how to deal with it." His caddie completed his thought, "He came to Firestone having done little actual practice, but from that point on, he had a mental image of himself that he was able to relate to the movement of his body." Tiger is using visualization techniques to stay at the top of his game. Now you can employ these same techniques in preparation for a deadly confrontation.

Visualization is nothing more than mental movie making. It is best done after relaxation has been induced through the previous relaxation techniques discussed. Once relaxed, begin to envision an incident that requires the self defense use of deadly force. A scenario that can be used is you and your spouse leave a restaurant in a downtown area. As you are walking to the car parked a block away, you approach a corner. A knife wielding thug jumps in front of you and demands your wallet. There is only about six feet separating you and your wife from this violent criminal.

Visualize engaging the robber in conversation by saying "Here it is. Take all of it, but please don't hurt us," as you reach toward your rear pocket. Draw your weapon and perform a perfect triple tap – two to center mass and one to the head.

Strive for involving all of your senses in this mental movie making. Feel the damp night air, smell the aromas coming from the surrounding restaurants, hear the traffic as it goes by on the street, see the violent criminal fall to the ground and no longer present a threat.

The more realistic you make your mental movie, the more training value it offers. Your body will experience the same physical changes caused by a real incident – heart rate increases, blood pressure increases, respirations increase, pupils dilate, etc. In fact, research has shown that athletes who imagine performing their sport causes electromyographical (EMG) activity in the musculature that resembles that which occurs when actually performing the physical skill. While the EMG increase seen during visualization is not as drastic as when performing the actual physical deed, it does increase. Therefore, visualization causes physical reactions in the body.

Since it is you directing your mental movie, it is important that during your visualization that you see yourself performing flawlessly. This is important because visualization works to the negative as well. That is, if technique is flawed or the outcome is less than satisfactory, you are conditioning yourself for potential failure. Because failure is not acceptable, do not let this happen in your v sualizations.

It is good to run different scenarios during subsequent visualization sessions. This is to ensure that you are not preparing for only one type of an event, such as the one given as an example here. Maybe the robber approaches from the rear, or there are two or three would be robbers, or the robber is armed with a handgun or crowbar. You get the point – variations should be visualized during different sessions.

Basically, there are three ways to visualize yourself in these types of scenarios. One process is called kenaesthesis, which is where someone actually feels the movements involved in the response internally. Next is called visual internal imagery, which is seeing your performance played back from your eyes' perspective. And finally, is the visual external imagery where you see yourself from a distance responding in the correct manner.

Personally, I use the visual internal imagery whereby I see the scenario unfold from my eyes' perspective. This simply is easiest for me. Experiment with each of the three ways to determine what works best for you.

Positive Self-Talk

Positive self-talk is nothing more than patting yourself on the back for a job well done. After your visualization session where you have seen yourself respond correctly, timely, and accurately in a given situation, then simply tell yourself how good a job you did in the scenario. Tell yourself, "I did a great job in identifying the dangerous situation and responded effectively to prevent my spouse and me from being victims!"

This positive self-talk reinforces what you did correctly and provides confidence that you can react in a similarly correct manner if faced with such a real-life altercation.

Tactical Awareness

Preparing mentally for a deadly encounter will help one survive a violent crime, but if one is unable to recognize the danger, quick reaction will not be forthcoming. One must truly live their day-by-day existence in a state of readiness in order to increase the odds of surviving a deadly force encounter. One way of living this is to ingrain awareness in oneself of your surroundings and be prepared to act decisively when the potential for an encounter is present. This awareness also minimizes one's chance of being victimized simply because the bad guys are looking for sheep who can easily be led to slaughter. Internalize this information to keep from being one of the sheep!

A simple color code system of awareness is a good way of internalizing the awareness mentality. This system is attributed to the U.S. Marine Corps developing it in World War II and to Jeff Cooper, who definitely made the color code system of awareness popular in self defense circles. Regardless of who came up with it, it is a way to monitor your awareness.

There are four stages of awareness – White, Yellow, Orange, and Red.

White – In color condition White a person is totally unprepared for any type of action, much less a deadly force encounter. Many people go through life in this condition. Think about a news story of someone involved in an accident saying "I didn't even see them."

As a devoted person reading this book and contemplating self protection, you should only find yourself in Condition White when at home, behind closed and locked doors. Condition White is when you are safely in your bed asleep, or engaging in other relaxation activities without the potential for any type of hostile encounter.

Yellow – Condition Yellow signifies general readiness. It is a type of relaxed alert. There are no specific threats, but you are aware of the world around you and the people and things in it. This particular condition is where you should find yourself about 99% of the time. This condition causes no extra stresses, but ensures you are scanning a 360 degree plane throughout your day. Definitely this is not a state of paranoia, just a restful awareness.

Predators look for the sheep that live in Condition White, but avoid those of us who live in Condition Yellow. Next time you are out and about, watch people around you. It will quickly become obvious who is aware of their surroundings and who is not. This is what predators look for before making their move. Always be alert and ready for action if needed!

Orange – One moves to Condition Orange when a specific alert has been identified. You may notice someone who is wearing a heavy jacket in the middle of summer, or has on a heavy toboggan that can easily be pulled down over the face to become a mask. It could be you notice two thugs closely watching an elderly lady with her arms full walking to her car. The thugs may choose to conduct a purse snatch or carjacking.

Basically, Condition Orange should be reached when something is out of place or just does not feel right. Follow your gut in determining escalation to this condition.

Red – Condition Red occurs when a threat presents itself and one should prepare to use deadly force to confront the threat. Recall the threat may not be directed at you, but a third person, such as the elderly lady mentioned before. Whatever the threat, your mental trigger has been tripped making you decide on an action to take.

This color code system is not to categorize danger, but rather to instill the mindset in you to prepare for a deadly force encounter. Many studies have been conducted on the readiness of a human being to kill another human being. All of these studies have revealed hesitancy in humans to kill other humans. A post World War II study determined a number of reasons the hit ratio during that war was no better than it actually was, but the primary reason was the hesitancy of the soldier to kill another human being.

Training of soldiers between World War II and Korea revealed that during the Korean, and even the Vietnam, wars soldiers became more predisposed to fire their weapons, but the hit ratio did not increase drastically. There is a basic human repugnance to the idea of killing another human being. In civilized society this is a very good thing, but you should keep in mind that this repugnance is a good thing only in rational, well adjusted humans. Unfortunately, the criminal element that you are preparing to protect yourself against does not fall into this category. Therefore, it is imperative that you mentally prepare yourself for taking a human life in self defense.

Your ability to take someone's life should be determined well before finding yourself in a position of using deadly force. General George Patton said it best, "The time to take counsel of your fears is before you make an important battle decision. That's the time to listen to every fear you can imagine! When you have collected all the facts and fears and made your decision, turn off all your fears and go ahead!"

Hopefully, this chapter helps in your personal endeavor of self protection.

Post Incident Mental Preparedness

Post-Traumatic Stress Disorder (PTSD) has become a commonly discussed issue in the news. Most often it is associated with military personnel following combat tours of duty. However, it can develop as a result of self defense encounters. Most often it results from a terrifying ordeal that involved harm or the threat of physical harm. Studies show that PTSD results from a variety of traumatic incidents such as assault, robbery, or rape (violent crime as defined previously). The PTSD victim may either have had the ordeal happen to themselves, to a loved one, or even to a stranger when they witnessed the event.

Symptoms displayed in PTSD victims include easily startled, emotionally numb, loss of interest in previously interesting things, problems showing affection, quickly become irritable, displays more aggression, or becomes violent. Every person faced with a traumatic ordeal does not develop PTSD; however, it is estimated that 7.7 million American adults suffer from PTSD. Symptoms generally develop within three months of the traumatic event. Statistics show that women are more susceptible to PTSD than men, but men do get PTSD.

Treatment is available should you find yourself a victim of PTSD following your deadly force encounter. The first person to see if you display any of the above symptoms following your incident is your family doctor. Your doctor can discuss your symptoms and determine if they are indeed a result of your incident and can refer you to the right mental health professional.

Bottom line – see a health care professional if you suspect PTSD following your incident. There is nothing to be ashamed of. It is a recognized problem that should be attended to. Do not survive the incident just to lose everything you stayed alive for. PTSD has an effect on your loved ones as well, and you owe it to them to seek help if you display these symptoms.

Chapter 8

Practicing for Self Defense

Owning a handgun doesn't make you armed any more than owning a guitar makes you a musician.
Jeff Cooper

What Jeff means by this quote is that owning a guitar does not make you a world class musician anymore than owning a gun makes you a world class marksman. Most who will read this book are not striving to be world class shooters, but do need the confidence that they can hit their target in a life or death situation. Practice is the only way to ensure that you can hit your target.

In my younger days when I was shooting competitively, I was shooting 250 rounds a week. During this time, I won many local and state practical pistol competitions (PPC). The Georgia Double Action course was the most popular in the state of Georgia at the time. It consisted of firing 50 rounds from the 3, 7, 15, and 25 yard lines. With the ball and dummy technique, however, I could actually fire the 50 round course at least twice per box of shells. Ball and dummy consists of loading a round every other chamber in the cylinder and then spinning the cylinder so you do not know when a round is going to fire. What this accomplishes is the ability to see if you are holding your weapon still when the hammer falls. You never know when the live round is going to line up, so it becomes necessary on every trigger press to hold the weapon steady. It seriously improves marksmanship skills.

I now shoot in local matches with my two sons, but am not into competitive shooting like then. My focus now is on defensive shooting. I shoot in International Defensive Pistol Association (IDPA) matches, and have recently begun shooting in United States Practical Shooting Association (USPSA) matches. Both of these two organizations are for defensive handgunners. These courses involve scenarios requiring competitors to employ defensive handgun skills. Stages of fire require tactical and emergency reloads, shoot and move, target differentiation (i.e., good guy, bad guy targets), accuracy, and speed. Normally, I fire my Glock 17.

These matches are excellent practice for the defensive handgunner looking to hone their skills. Find a local club and begin shooting in these types of competitions. The added stress induced by competition will serve you well if ever faced with a defensive shooting situation.

In the meantime, I cannot stress how important practice is. Many will ask how much practice is necessary. The answer is that it depends on your current skills. Obviously, the more practice the better, but even after not competing for 20 years, the skills I developed when shooting in competition have remained – I can still hit my target. I may not be as strong, fast, steady, or have the eyesight I once did, but for defensive work I am fully confident in my ability to hit my target. This is the confidence you need to develop in your practice. So to answer the question how much practice should you do, practice until you feel confident that you can draw, acquire the target, and deliver three accurate rounds within a minimum of five seconds. When you can accomplish this, then you can cut back on your practice sessions because you have developed the skills necessary for defensive handgun work. Notice I did not say stop practicing, I simply said cut back on your practice sessions.

In this chapter we will discuss practice ammunition, inexpensive targets, and a series of courses of fire that should be in everyone's practice routine.

Practice Ammunition

Really, the only word on practice ammunition is that it should replicate the power of your regular carry ammunition. For instance, I carry a 125 grain jacketed hollow point (JHP) in my Glock 17 for defensive work, so I practice with 125 grain full metal jacket (FMJ) ammunition. The FMJ is less expensive to buy than the JHP; however, when I reload my practice ammunition I use 125 grain JHP. For bulk purchase of bullets, there is not much difference in the price. These practice rounds provide the same bullet weight, powder charge, velocity, and recoil as my carry rounds. This is what you should strive for in your practice ammunition, as well.

Realistic Practice Targets

Targets are really not that expensive to buy, when buying in bulk (e.g., 100 targets or more). There are many types of targets available. There are color realistic targets, black and white silhouette targets, color silhouette targets, and cardboard targets like the IDPA target depicted here.

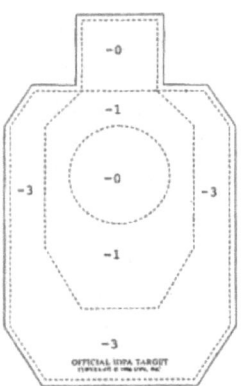

Figure 14 – IDPA Cardboard Target

Depending on the system to hold the target in use at the range, cardboard backing is required to attach the target.

The IDPA targets, however, are already cardboard and do not require a separate cardboard backing. These can be bought in bulk at reasonable prices. But there is a less expensive option for IDPA type targets with the origin being your supermarket.

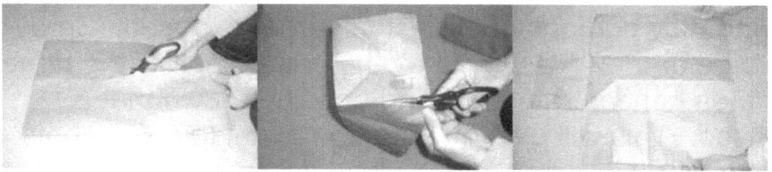

Photo 8 – Free Targets

In the future when you buy groceries ask for paper shopping bags instead of plastic. These paper bags can easily be fashioned into IDPA type targets. To turn paper grocery bags into IDPA targets, simply refold the bag flat as it was before it was used. Take a pair of scissors and cut the bag in half lengthwise (left photo). Fold the bottom out and cut the bottom of the bag from middle to corner along the two side seams (middle photo). Then fold the remaining center piece up (right photo). You now have a free IDPA type target. The official IDPA target measures 18.75" by 30.75"; whereas, our free grocery bag target measures 18.875" by 23". The free target is shorter, but about the same width as the IDPA target. These can be stapled to cardboard backing at the range.

As you can see from Figure 14, the IDPA target has perforations indicating the scoring rings. These scoring rings obviously will not be present on the grocery bag targets, but one can simply take a nine inch paper plate and a child's buff colored crayon and trace the plate in the center mass area to give a scoring ring. For practice purposes, one should only be interested in center mass for scoring.

Inexpensive, flimsy nine inch paper plates can be stapled over the center of the target to provide a clean impact target for subsequent shots.

To add realism to any of these targets during practice, take an old tee shirt that was going to be thrown away anyway and drape it over the head of the target. Now even the scoring rings are obscured from your vision and a more realistic look is provided for practice.

Targets can be spray painted to indicate hard cover leaving only portions of the actual target exposed. Spray one side or the other, or spray the bottom half of the target, and then concentrate on hitting only the brown that is exposed. This will get you used to having to place shots more accurately when faced with a bad guy using cover or concealment.

Courses of Fire

In Chapter 6 I explained the Defensive Handgun Triad (Accuracy, Power, and Speed). Power is already taken care of with the selection of your defensive handgun. That leaves accuracy and speed. When first beginning your practice sessions, the focus should be on accuracy. Only after becoming accurate can one work on speed. Sure you want to shoot as fast as you can, but as fast as you can means as fast as you are accurate. One solid hit means much more than 17 close misses. In defensive handgun, real world incidents of "spray and pray" have no place. Only good solid hits will take your adversary out of the fight.

The courses of fire that I am presenting here are basic in nature. They work on the fundamentals of gun handling so you can develop your skills. I, obviously, would not suggest you load your 17 round magazine with only six rounds when carrying for defense purposes; however, by doing this during practice sessions you are able to work on tactical and emergency reloading, as well as marksmanship.

Remember to find out the local range rules and abide by them at all times. These should always be in addition to the Four Commandments previously discussed in regards to firearms safety.

Most of these courses of fire are scenario based. They come from actual street incidents that a defensive handgunner may be involved. As you practice more you will come up with your own scenarios. Until then, I am providing some useful scenarios for your use.

Georgia Semi-Auto Pistol Qualification Course

When first starting your practice, it is a good thing to fire a qualification course of fire for score. Then later in your skill development you can fire the course again to determine your degree of improvement. With this said, I am not a big believer in standard qualification courses of fire. They typically do not cover all the skills that a defensive handgunner needs to develop; however, they are good for being consistent in providing a score by which one can compare oneself to previous qualification efforts.

This standard qualification course is taken from Georgia. I have modified this course of fire for purposes of this book. All states have mandated qualification courses that police officers typically are required to fire at least once a year for record. Most state courses are similar. Many have their own target requirements, which are not necessary for giving yourself an idea of your ability. I suggest using the IDPA target previously shown or using your inexpensive shopping bag target. Scoring can be easily enough done on either. Using the IDPA target, count all hits in the -0 and -1 rings as 10, with all -3 hits counting 8. On the shopping bag target, estimate your hit score.

This course of fire requires 30 rounds of ammunition. Two targets are required to be set up at equal distances with one foot separating them. Magazines shall always be loaded with six rounds. All required reloads are the shooter's responsibility. Any malfunctions encountered must be cleared. Maximum raw score for this course of fire on the IDPA target is 300 and the minimum qualifying score is 240 (80%). The following are the stages of fire:

Stage One: 25 yard line, left side behind cover, weapon out, two-hand grip, on command:
Fire 1 round in 4 seconds at right target center mass and return to cover
Fire 1 round in 4 seconds at left target center mass and return to cover and holster

Right side behind cover, weapon out, two-hand grip, on command:

Fire 1 round in 4 seconds at left target center mass and return to cover
Fire 1 round in 4 seconds at right target center mass and return to cover and holster

Stage Two: 15 yard line standing outside cover facing targets with weapon holstered, on command move behind cover and fire 4 rounds in 12 seconds in the following manner:

1 round at right target center mass
1 round at left target center mass

Drop to kneeling position

1 round at right target center mass
1 round at left target center mass and holster

Stage Thee: 7 yard line standing with weapon holstered on command draw and fire 4 rounds in 5 seconds in the following manner:

2 rounds at right target center mass
2 rounds at left target center mass

Reload and holster (Reload 2 magazines with 6 rounds)

Standing in front of right target, on command draw and fire 2 rounds at right target center mass, move one step left and fire 2 rounds at right target center mass in 6 seconds and holster

Standing in front of left target, on command draw and fire 2 rounds at left target center mass, move one step right, reload and fire 2 rounds at left target center mass in 12 seconds and holster

From a low ready position (weapon out and pointing at, but below the target, fire a failure drill (head shots), 2 rounds in 3 seconds into the head

1 round right target head shot
1 round left target head shot and holster

Stage Four: 3 yard line, on command, draw while taking one step back and giving verbal commands, fire 2 rounds in 3 seconds

1 round right target center mass
1 round left target center mass

Reload and holster

On command, draw while taking one step back and giving verbal commands, fire 4 rounds in 5 seconds

2 rounds right target center mass
2 rounds left target center mass

Come to high ready position, evaluating targets

On command fire 2 rounds in 2 seconds

1 round right target center mass
1 round left target center mass

Clear and holster an empty weapon

During this course of fire, 30 rounds have been expended. Reloading has been required. The use of cover and movement has been incorporated. Failure drills with head shots have been fired. Creating distance and verbal commands have been used. While a short qualification course, it has incorporated a number of techniques discussed in Chapter 6.

Scoring of Scenarios

The following courses of fire are all scenario based. That is, I provide a quick briefing of what has or is taking place. Target setup and shooter location is depicted. There are no time limits. Shoot until the problem is solved. However, if someone is with you during your practice sessions, have them time you during these scenarios, so as to allow for scoring of the course of fire. I have provided a Par Time, which is a time that you should attempt to complete the scenario in.

The IDPA target and scoring system is designed to reward accuracy over pure speed, which is as it should be. The Vickers Count scoring system is used, which converts everything to a time score with the fastest time being best. This is a way of marking your progress in subsequent practice sessions. A scoring sheet or sheet of paper will be necessary to keep track of your score. Buying a journal at an office supply store can be useful in tracking your progress. The following is the easiest way to score a Vickers Count:

1. First, write down the time it took to complete the course or stage of fire.
2. Next, score the target and count the total number of misses. Then multiply the total number of misses by five (5) points.
4. Next, count the number of points down for the remaining shots and multiply this number by half (.5) seconds.
5. Add the raw time to the converted points down for a final score.
6. Now everything has been converted to time so that the lowest (fastest) time wins.

SCORING EXAMPLE:

Let us suppose that a course of fire consists of a total of three targets with two shots on each and it takes you 12 seconds to complete this course of fire and you have four -0 and 2 -1. The following is how to score it using the Vickers Count:

Time:_____12_____

Misses:_____0 x 5 = 0_____

Points
Down:_____2 x .5 = 1_____

Final
Score:_____13_____

The next time you fire this same course, you should strive for a lower score than 13. This can be accomplished two ways – place all six rounds in the -0 or maintain the same hit count only with a faster time. The following are example scenario drills.

Two Thugs

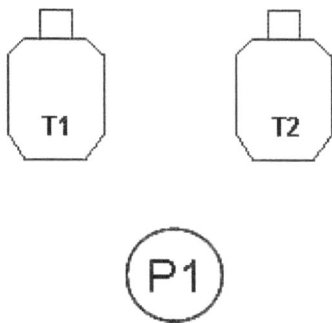

Figure 15 – Two Thugs

Round Count: 4 rounds
Target Distance: Three yards
Targets Required: Two threat targets
Scoring Method: Par time 8 seconds
Starting Position/Hand Position: Weapon holstered standing
Start Signal: On Command
Stop Signal: Last shot fired

Scenario: You are walking down the sidewalk at night when two thugs step in front of you. One thug (T1) says he is going to kill you and take your wallet. He reaches into his rear pocket and comes out with a small handgun and begins to bring it up in your direction.

Procedure: On signal, draw and fire two rounds center mass at T1. Scan. The second thug (T2) pulls a butcher knife out and begins to move toward you. Fire two rounds center mass at T2.
* NOTE: P1 is Shooter Position One.

Loved One Hostage

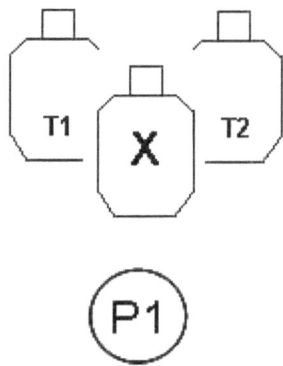

Figure 16 – Loved One Hostage

Round Count: 6 rounds
Target Distance: 7 yards
Targets Required: Two threat targets, one hostage target
Scoring Method: Par time 10 seconds
Starting Position/Hand Position: Hand on holstered weapon
Start Signal: On Command
Stop Signal: Last shot fired

Scenario: You and your wife are walking to a downtown restaurant. Two males come out behind you. One grabs your wife and the two of them back away and demand all your valuables or they threaten to kill your wife. One bad guy (T2) pulls a knife and holds it out to his side.

Procedure: At the start signal, engage in tactical priority (T2 and then T1) with two rounds to the body and one shot to the head on both targets.

Transition Drill

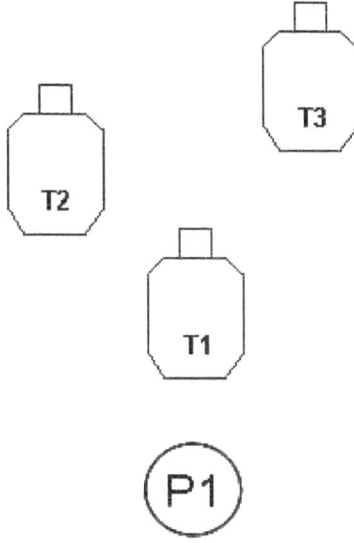

Figure 17 – Transition Drill

Round Count: 6 rounds
Target Distance: T1 = 7 Yards, T2 = 10 Yards, and T3 = 13 Yards
Targets Required: Three threat targets
Scoring Method: Par time 12 seconds
Starting Position/Hand Position: Weapon in low ready
Start Signal: On Command
Stop Signal: Last shot fired

Scenario: You are talking to three trespassers who have wandered onto your back deck. While talking to them T3 pulls a handgun and begins to point at you.

Procedure: Engage T3 with two rounds center mass and Scan. T1 has picked up a baseball bat and is rushing at you, Engage T1 with two rounds center mass and Scan. T2 has pulled a knife from his pocket and is running toward you. Engage T2 with two rounds center mass and Scan.

Car Defense

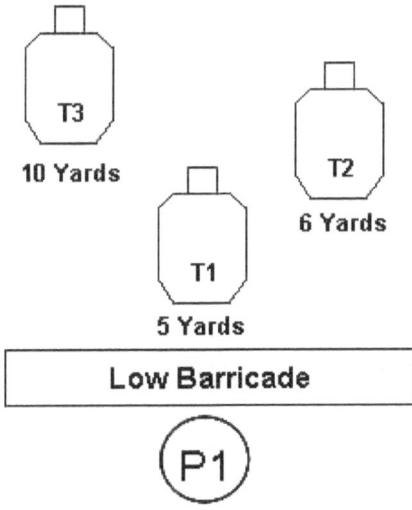

Figure 18 – Car Defense

Round Count: 6 rounds
Target Distance: T1 = 5 Yards, T2 = 6 Yards, T3 =10 Yards
Targets Required: Three threat targets
Scoring Method: Par time 12 seconds
Starting Position/Hand Position: Simulate one hand on steering wheel and other hand on ignition switch
Start Signal: Weapon Holstered On Command
Stop Signal: Last shot fired

Scenario: Having just entered your car at the mall, you are starting your car when you notice three armed suspects rapidly approaching your car. The lead suspect (T1) is armed with a shotgun that he is raising in your direction. The other two suspects are armed with handguns.

Procedure: Begin with one magazine fully loaded, weapon holstered, sitting in a chair with left side toward targets. At the start signal, engage targets in tactical priority (heaviest armed, closest) with two shots each to center mass.

Axis of Attack

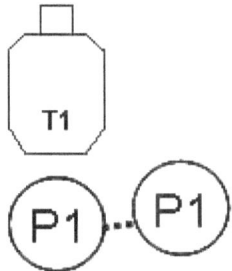

Figure 19 – Axis of Attack

Round Count: 3 rounds
Target Distance: Arms Length
Targets Required: One threat target
Scoring Method: Par time 5 seconds
Starting Position/Hand Position: Weapon Holstered Arms by Side
Start Signal: On Command
Stop Signal: Last shot fired

Scenario: You have been stopped by what appears to be a panhandler. While talking to the person, he reaches into his pocket, pulls a knife, and begins moving at you very quickly.

Procedure: Begin with magazine fully loaded. On Command, throw your weak hand at the head of the target, take one step to the right, and draw weapon all simultaneously. Move weak hand out of the way, fire two rounds at center mass. You notice the suspect is still moving at you as though the two rounds have not fazed him. Fire one round at the head.

CAUTION: Be aware of your weak hand and do not cross it with the muzzle of your weapon!

At Home In Bed

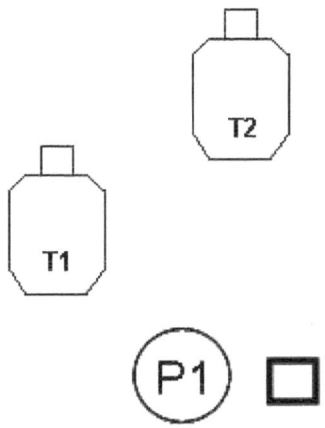

Figure 20 – At Home in Bed

Round Count: 6 rounds
Target Distance: T1 = 3 Yards, T2 = 7 Yards
Targets Required: Two threat targets
Scoring Method: Par time 12 seconds
Starting Position/Hand Position: Weapon Lying on Table Next to Shooter (Shooter can lie down as though in bed)
Start Signal: On Command
Stop Signal: Last shot fired

Scenario: While asleep one night, you hear breaking glass in the front of your house. You awake and see two unknown males standing in your bedroom. One is holding a crowbar and the other is holding a baseball bat.

Procedure: Begin with magazine fully loaded and weapon lying on table. On Command, reach for your weapon and fire two rounds in each target in tactical priority (nearest first). After firing at both targets, neither has gone down. Fire one round in the head of each target.

Shoot and Move/Malfunction

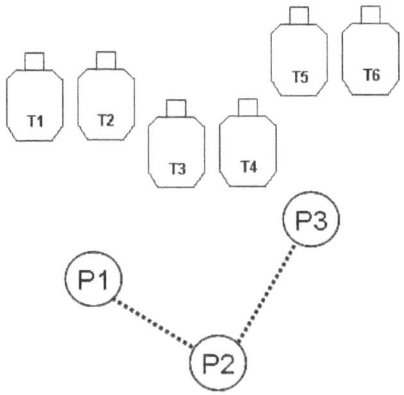

Figure 21 – Shoot and Move/Malfunction

Round Count: 12 rounds
Target Distance: T1 & T2 = 5 Yards, T3 & T4 = 10 Yards,
T5 & T6 = 7 Yards
Targets Required: Six threat targets
Scoring Method: Par time 30 seconds
Starting Position/Hand Position: Weapon Holstered and
Two Magazines
Start Signal: On Command
Stop Signal: Last shot fired

Scenario: While walking home one night, you find yourself
in the middle of a gang shootout.

Procedure: Begin with one magazine loaded with nine live
rounds and one spent round inserted in the middle of the
magazine, and a second magazine loaded with 10 live
rounds. Have someone other than the shooter to load the
magazine so the shooter does not know when the
malfunction will occur. On Command, fire two rounds at
both T1 and T2 (four rounds total) and move to P2. Fire two
rounds at both T3 and T4 (four rounds total) and move to P3.

Fire two rounds at both T5 and T6 (four rounds total), scan and reholster. Clear the malfunction whenever it occurs.

SUMMARY

These seven examples of scenarios for practice are simple to set up and run. They cover the basics of accuracy, power and speed. Tactics and techniques discussed in Chapter 6 come into play in these scenarios. Real world cases similar to these practice scenarios victimize Americans everyday. You must take your practice serious and incorporate scenario training such as these into your marksmanship training.

Use news stories of violent crime in your area to develop your own scenarios in future training sessions. Strive for accuracy and speed. Continue to track your progress. Incorporate your scenario training into your mental preparedness sessions, and be sure to tell yourself when you do a good job. All of this combined will ensure your success when faced with violent criminals who are intent on harming you or your family.

Chapter 9

Surviving the
Post Shooting Investigation

The right of self defense never ceases. It is among the most sacred, and alike necessary to nations and to individuals....

James Monroe
5Th President of the
United States

Several years ago in my hometown, a well respected local businessman shot and killed a former employee. It seems the former employee thought his former boss would be an easy mark for a home invasion robbery. The homeowner and his wife were in the house when they heard a noise at the back door. Retrieving a handgun, the homeowner went to investigate the noise. What he found was someone dressed in dark clothing trying to pry his kitchen door open. When he verbally challenged the would be robber, the robber pulled a handgun and pointed at the owner, who then raised his weapon and shot the intruder through the door, killing him. No charges were brought against the homeowner – it was a clear cut case of self defense.

More recently in Missouri, an individual was acquitted of a self defense shooting. Apparently, the two combatants had engaged in a verbal confrontation. One threatened to get his gun and shoot the other. Later in the parking lot, the combatant who made the threat approached the other and continued the verbal assault. At some point, the antagonizer reached into his back waistband as though going for a gun.

The self defender pulled his weapon out, fired and killed his assaulter. He was prosecuted for manslaughter, but a jury acquitted him on the grounds of self defense.

What is the difference in these two incidents? Obviously, a home defense is easier for law enforcement to identify as a self defense shooting than is an altercation that continues over a period of time, but a number of factors come into play w th regards to prosecuting the self defense shooter. All must remember that the decision to prosecute is that of the local prosecuting attorney, who is an elected official. One case may have occurred in a gun friendly jurisdiction, while the other was in a more gun restrictive environment. As in most governmental decisions, politics will come into play.

Unfortunately when the shooting has stopped and the gun smoke has cleared, anyone using deadly force in self defense must then be prepared for the investigation to come. Realize that when the police arrive on scene there will be a body lying on the ground and a shooter still alive. It can easily be perceived that the dead guy is the victim in all of this. What is one to do when faced with this situation? That is the purpose of this chapter of the book. I do not want any of my readers to survive a deadly encounter on the street just to be unjustly convicted of murder, manslaughter, or other crime.

A number of scientific studies have been conducted of law enforcement officers after they have been involved in deadly shootouts with bad guys. The results of these studies have led law enforcement administrators to issue new policies on how to handle officers post-shooting with regard to the required investigation. Police involved in self defense deadly force encounters are no different than the average citizen who finds themselves involved in this type of tragic situation. In fact, police officers should be better prepared than the average citizen because of the training they receive. I will explain these new policies and how you can use them to your advantage immediately after a shooting event.

Everyone has heard the term "I'll take the fifth." This refers to the U.S. Constitution's Fifth Amendment rights against self incrimination. I will discuss this right and all the ramifications it has with regard to the citizen self defender. Our forefathers over a long period of time drafted these amendments so that "we the people" can be safe from government oppression. They are our rights to be exercised – not to be dismissed because they do not fall into a detective's plan for case clearance.

Finally, in this chapter I will provide an easy to follow game plan for managing a post shooting situation. Like all else discussed in this book it will require practice on your part to get the script right after having experienced the high stress of a deadly force encounter. It is not intended to mislead anyone in its detail, but rather to get the point across that you were acting in self defense.

Research Results

There has been a lot of research conducted on post shooting perceptions. We discussed in Chapter 7 the physical impact of increased heart rate, blood pressure, tunnel vision and auditory perception. I shared with you my personal results with regard to these phenomena. Here I will provide thumbnail sketches of some of the more prevalent research results.

1986 Study

In 1986, researchers R.M. Solomon and J.M. Horn published the results of their study for Psychological Services for Law Enforcement in an article entitled, "Post-Shooting Traumatic Reactions: A Pilot Study." There were 86 officers involved in this study who had lived through a deadly force encounter. What they found was that officers experienced visual and auditory distortions in the following number of cases:

Number of Officers in Study: 86
Visual Perception:
     Slow Motion: 67%
     Faster than Normal: 15%
     Tunnel Vision: 37%
     Greater Visual Detail: 18%
Auditory Perception:
     Sounds Diminished: 51%
     Sounds Intensified: 18%

1998 Report

A 1998 research project conducted by A.L. Hoenig and J.E. Roland was reported on in the October 1998 Police Chief magazine. Their article was entitled, "Shots Fired: Officer Involved." Following are the results of that study.

Number of Officers in Study: 348
Visual Perception:
     Slow Motion: 41%
     Faster than Normal: 20%
     Tunnel Vision: 45%
     Greater Visual Detail: 41%
Auditory Perception:
     Sounds Diminished: 51%
     Sounds Intensified: 23%
Memory Loss: 22%

2001 Report

In 2001, David Klinger in the U.S. Department of Justice, National Institute of Justice report, "Police Responses to Officer-Involved Shootings" provided details of his government funded research project. While all results do not total 100%, and some actually go above 100%, there were 80 officers interviewed who had been involved in 113 separate cases. Consequently, officers could have experienced different stimuli during different incidents. Following are the results of that study:

Number of Officers in Study: 80
Visual Perception:
      Slow Motion: 56%
      Faster than Normal: 23%
      Tunnel Vision: 51%
      Greater Visual Detail: 56%
Auditory Perception:
      Sounds Diminished: 82%
      Sounds Intensified: 20%
Memory Loss: Not Available

2002 Report

Dr. Alexis Artwohl reported in her article "Perceptual and Memory Distortion During Officer-Involved Shootings" published in the October 2002 FBI Bulletin her research results. Following are her results:

Number of Officers in Study: 157
Visual Perception:
      Slow Motion: 62%
      Faster than Normal: 17%
      Tunnel Vision: 79%
      Greater Visual Detail: 71%
Auditory Perception:
      Sounds Diminished: 84%
      Sounds Intensified: 16%
Memory Loss: 52% part of event, 46% for own behavior
Memory Distortion (saw or heard something that didn't happen): 21%
Dissociation (Detachment or unreality): 39%
Temporary Paralysis (Did not act): 7%

What do these studies have to do with the civilian defensive handgunner? They provide concrete, scientific evidence that people involved in gunfights with bad guys suffer from perceptual distortion. Consequently, if you are involved in a self defense use of a firearm, you too will most likely suffer some of these perceptual problems. What this should tell you is to listen when I provide a common sense process to follow after a self defense shooting. By doing so, you just may be doing yourself and your attorney a favor.

Law Enforcement Policies Have Changed

Based on studies such as these, law enforcement administrators have changed policies on how to deal with officers after an officer involved shooting. In 2004 the International Association of Chiefs of Police (IACP) issued an "Officer Involved Shooting Guideline." In addition to calling for officer training in acute stress and traumatic reactions, it calls for establishing relations with trained mental health professionals to work with officers post-shooting. Furthermore, it calls for proceduralizing how post shooting investigations will be conducted and on requiring post-shooting interventions. However, more importantly, it discusses what should occur immediately following a shooting incident.

IACP's guidelines state that an officer should be offered "an opportunity to step away from the scene and away from media attention by waiting at a remote location." It further states that on-scene personnel "should help the officer follow departmental policies regarding talking about the incident before the initial investigation interviews." Furthermore, it speaks to what should be done if the officer feels the immediate need to talk about the incident by stating the officer "should be provided with a resource that offers the officer confidentiality or privileged communications."

The reason IACP believes an officer should be provided "confidentiality or privileged communications" immediately following the incident is because they are aware of the perceptual distortions that occur during an officer involved shooting. Therefore, they are trying to protect against any of these distortions being used against the officer at a later time when, most likely, the story will become more clear and accurate as to what happened.

This model guideline goes further in discussion of when and how the initial investigative interview should occur by stating, "Ideally, the officer should be provided with some recovery time before detailed interviewing begins. This can range from a few hours to overnight. Officers who have been afforded this opportunity are likely to provide a more coherent and accurate statement. Providing a secure setting, insulated from the press and curious officers, is desirable during the interview process."

Unfortunately, these guidelines do not apply to the citizen who has just acted in self defense, but the citizen should learn from the facts provided in the previous research synopses and this IACP guideline. Perceptual distortions occur in a majority of self defense shootings, and other research studies have shown that a cool down period should be allowed before a detailed investigative interview occurs. While citizens are not covered by the IACP guidelines, they are, fortunately, covered by the Fifth Amendment to the United States Constitution!

Fifth Amendment Rights

I am sure everyone reading this book has heard the term "I'll take the fifth." But what does this mean? It means that you will not self-incriminate yourself by talking about something you are being investigated for.

Again, I am sure everyone is familiar with Miranda Rights. If you have ever watched a weekly cop show or movie, you would have heard of Miranda Rights. For the sake of clarity, however, the following is a sample Miranda Right statement given by police:

- You have the right to remain silent.
- Anything you say can and will be used against you in a court of law.
- You have the right to speak to an attorney, and to have an attorney present during any questioning.
- If you cannot afford an attorney, one will be provided for you free of charge.

Then the officer will ask, "Do you understand these rights? Do you want to talk to me about this incident?"

All police agencies may not use this exact wording, but the major parts will all be covered. The courts do not require these rights to appear verbatim to these. An officer can deviate from these exact phrases, but must cover all the points and be able to testify verbatim as to what exactly it was they said to you about your rights.

If you are not a member of the legal profession, then you most likely do not understand that Miranda Right Warnings are not required to be given except in custodial interrogatories. That is, when the first officer arrives on the scene following a self defense shooting, whatever is said by you can and will be used against you in court. Any statements made by you are admissible in court because they are considered "threshold statements." Threshold statements are made before any facts are known. In fact, an officer can ask questions initially to determine the nature of the call. Any answers to these questions are admissible in court. Again, they are threshold in nature. It is not until you have either been taken into custody or been detained are law enforcement officers required to give you your Miranda Rights, but only if they are asking questions is it necessary.

A tactic used by law enforcement is to place someone under arrest, put them in a patrol car, and transport them to the police station. The officer transporting the suspect is told not to ask any questions or to talk to the suspect. Suspects often say a lot of things in an effort to gain their freedom. Police only have to listen. Many statements are indeed incriminating and can be used without giving a Miranda Warning as long as law enforcement officers are not asking questions.

When the first police officer arrives on scene, they do not know the facts as you do. It is common nature to tell your side of the story, but you must remember the perceptual distortions that most likely have occurred may make you provide comments that are factually incorrect, which will become a problem for you later in the investigation.

This is a very difficult position to be placed in on top of the stress and potential trauma that you have endured during this self defense situation. Consider the police officer's position though. They have received a call about a gunshot wound. They arrive on scene to find one person down and another alive with a weapon. It can be easy for the officer to immediately misclassify victim and perpetrator. It also can be easy to totally get these two reversed – you are the victim and the down guy is the perpetrator, but unfortunately this is not the way it typically works out for the police. Therefore, you will have to say something, but that something should be well thought out before speaking to police, and only then should minimum details be provided at that specific time.

John Farnam, a well respected firearms/defensive tactics instructor, is often called as an expert witness in self defense shootings. He advises defense attorneys representing self defense shooters. This is one of his quotes, "The most dangerous and damaging single thing one can do in the wake of a lethal confrontation, the one act that fatally damages most claims of legitimate self-defense? Answering questions asked by police investigators, at the scene, without first insisting on having your attorney present."

There is no shame in exercising your Fifth Amendment Rights following a shooting incident. By so doing you will provide yourself the best opportunity to prove yourself innocent of any criminal conduct.

Post Shooting Game Plan

Realizing the perceptual distortions that will occur and your personal right to not self-incriminate, you need to have a game plan for dealing with the police after a self defense shooting. The plan will entail securing the scene, checking yourself for injury, notifying police, and what to say when police arrive. More detail on each of these is discussed below.

Secure The Scene

After your attacker has gone down, you should scan the area to ensure no other threats are present. If your attacker had a weapon, you should move it out of reach of the attacker. Be aware that by moving the attacker's weapon overzealous law enforcement may consider this evidence tampering. But your reason for moving it is that you are not a trained medical professional who can determine that death has indeed occurred; therefore, you moved the attacker's weapon out of their reach to ensure they no longer presented a threat to you or other nearby innocent people.

Once the scene is secure, check yourself out for any injuries. If anyone was with you, ensure they are injury free, as well. If there are injuries, begin first aid based on your experience and training. If the attacker was armed, you may have injuries you are not aware of, so conduct a head to toe check. Should you be injured, then seek medical attention. However, do not fake injuries to buy time before facing police. This will be seen as being deceitful and may cause the police to view any future statements skeptically. Sign of deceit in one area typically portends deceit in other areas. Do not give police a reason not to believe your story.

Call Police

Police must be called and informed of the incident. A

bystander may have already called, but the only way to be certain is to either call police yourself or ask someone else to call them. Regardless of who calls the police, the phone call will be recorded and can be used in court at some point in the future.

Not knowing who may have called or what they might have said, I would recommend calling the police yourself. By doing this you begin to give your side of the story immediately, but caution should be shown in the dialog between yourself and the 911 operator. The following is what should be relayed to the 911 operator:

- My name is _____.

- I was attacked (robbed, assaulted, raped, shot, or whatever).

- I was in fear of my life and defended myself. I need an ambulance and police at _____.

- If there were more than one attacker and an attacker ran from the scene, then a description of this attacker and his direction of travel should be given to the 911 operator.

911 operators will most likely ask you questions that are open ended (i.e., requiring more than a yes or no answer). Do not answer these questions, and do not elaborate. The minimal information above is sufficient for 911 operators to dispatch an ambulance and police. DO NOT OFFER MORE INFORMATION THAN NECESSARY!

It goes without saying that you should stay at the scene until police arrive. The only acceptable reason for leaving the scene is to seek medical help for you or a loved one who has been seriously injured. In this event, call police and give the information above and tell them where you will be.

I realize that telling you to stay at the scene is nothing more than common sense. However, there are many instances where legitimate self defense shooters have left the scene without notifying police of the incident. Police will be notified, so an investigation will begin. Think about it. If the guy who did the shooting left the scene and did not contact police, could this be seen as being deceitful? Of course it could. In such incidents the self defender may be tried and acquitted. But if they had notified police and stayed at the scene, most likely they would not have been charged in the first place. Therefore, do not let post-incident stress cloud your judgment. Call the police, provide minimal details, and stay at the scene!

When Police Arrive

After securing the scene and calling police, next you should prepare for their arrival. First, holster your weapon. The last thing you want is the police arriving to find an armed person that they must deal with. Present the least threatening appearance possible. When the first officer arrives, clearly show him two empty hands and follow any instructions he may give you. Expect to have your handgun taken from you. Most likely police will keep your handgun until the investigation is complete. If you are charged with a crime, your weapon is evidence and will be kept until the trial is finished.

Because of the appearance of the scene, a dead bad guy who police do not know is a bad guy, and a live good guy, again, that the police do not know is the good guy, a short statement should be made. It should go like this:

> "He (she or they) attacked (robbed, raped, assaulted or whatever happened) me and I acted in self defense."

This clearly states what happened without providing too much detail at this time. It places the police on notice that this was a crime perpetrated against an armed citizen.

The next statement should be:

"I will press charges against my attacker."

What this statement does is speak a language the officer understands – that the victim is willing to go through the legal process for ensuring the bad guy is punished by the legal system.

If there were any witnesses to the incident, you should point these people out to the officer. Many witnesses are not interested in getting involved and may have to be persuaded to do so. Tell the officer:

"That person, or those people, saw it all. You need to get their names and interview them as to what they saw."

By pointing out the witnesses, you appear to be helping the officer, which you are. But you are also putting police on notice that there are witnesses that can be called upon to support your side of the story. This will make them more cautious about jumping to conclusions.

Additionally, if there is any evidence present, point it out to the officer. For instance, the attacker's weapon that you moved away from their reach when securing the scene, you can say:

"Officer, after my attacker went down, I moved his weapon out of his reach to further protect me and other innocents. It is right there."

Again, you are being helpful to the police and have given the reason why the weapon will have your fingerprints on it.

After your two statements and helpful direction to

witnesses and evidence, you should make this statement:

> "Officer I am willing to fully cooperate in your investigation. I will answer all questions after I have talked to my lawyer."

By this statement you are assuring police that you will help in their investigation, but you want to have a lawyer before you answer any questions.

Many officers will persist in asking questions. In fact, you may get a number of questions as a result of your previous statements and pointing out evidentiary people and items. However, do not fall into the trap of saying too much. These minimal statements should suffice until you have had time to confer with an attorney. If the officer says something like "So you are going to lawyer up. What do you have to hide?" You simply answer "I have nothing to hide, but I am exercising my Fifth Amendment rights. I would like to talk to my attorney now."

Most likely the first officer on the scene will not be the investigator. Eventually a detective will arrive on the scene to take over the investigation. The detective will be briefed by the officer you made your statements to, and then will most likely come to talk with you. If the detective does not read you your Miranda Warning, but starts to ask you questions. You can ask if you are free to leave. If you are told no, then you are under detention. In which case, Miranda rights apply to any questions asked by the detective. Regardless, when the detective asks you the first question, reiterate that you will fully cooperate after conferring with your lawyer. At this point the detective will either stop talking to you, or will try to persuade you to talk more.

Now you must be extra careful. Do not answer detail oriented questions. It is safe to give your name, address, and telephone number, but do not go further. If the officer asks if this was an accidental shooting, tell him you want your lawyer. If he asks how close you were when you fired, tell him you want your lawyer. Do not be shy about asking for an attorney. Do not ask the detective if you need an attorney. You do need an attorney, so demand to see one and do not answer questions until you have seen the attorney.

An attorney will tell you not to answer any questions, so do not answer questions until you have had the opportunity to talk to an attorney.

You should fully expect detention when you refuse to answer questions, but do not answer without an attorney present!

In summary, realize that perceptual distortion will occur during a stressful defense shooting. Details will not be what you should talk about immediately following a defensive shooting. Provide minimal information when relaying details immediately following a shooting incident. Exercise your Fifth Amendment rights and demand to have an attorney before giving details of the incident. Be non-threatening, helpful, and non-committal during your first encounter with law enforcement following a defensive shooting incident. Be cooperative, but insist on having an attorney present during and interview/interrogation following your event. Don't survive the deadly force encounter to only be persecuted during the follow on investigation!

Chapter 10

Concealed Carry Law

Firearms are second only to the Constitution in importance; they are the peoples' liberty's teeth.
George Washington

This year will go down in history. For the first time, a civilized nation has full gun registration. Our streets will be safer, our police more efficient, and the world will follow our lead into the future!"
Adolph Hitler, 1933

Our founding fathers of the United States of America knew that in order to remain a free and civil society the people needed the freedom to own and bear arms. This is fully documented in the Federalist Papers, the Second Amendment to the United States Constitution, and many other documents penned by our founding fathers.

There are many who would severely limit or outright rescind this individual right. As seen in the quote by Adolph Hitler from 1933, gun control has been tried in other free nations, but has always resulted in reduced personal rights.

I recall reading a letter to the editor in my local newspaper when I was just a teenager. The writer was a World War II veteran who had been involved in interrogating high level German officers following the war. He recalled one high ranking German officer telling his interrogators that Germany had considered invading the United States during the war, but decided against it because of the freedom of the people to own firearms. Germany expected they would have gotten entrenched in guerrilla fighting with armed United

148

States citizens. This kept Germany from invading. How many other countries or terrorist organizations are afraid of invading the United States because of the freedom of gun ownership?

The Second Amendment to the United States Constitution reads:

> *A well regulated Militia, being necessary to the security of a Free State, the right of the people to keep and bear Arms, shall not be infringed.*

It is this, the second freedom espoused in the Bill of Rights that guarantees American citizens the right to own firearms. As a committed defensive handgunner, one must remain vigilant about one's rights. Many proponents of gun control insist that the Second Amendment is a collective state right versus an individual right. Fortunately, the Supreme Court ruled in 2008, again, in the District of Columbia vs. Heller that the right to own and bear arms was an individual right.

There are proponents of gun control who believe that societies with strict gun control or that outright outlaw individual gun ownership are more civil and have lower crime rates than the United States. This too, is untrue. In comparing violent crime rates between England and the United States, one finds that England has a much higher violent crime rate than does the United States. When the entire European Union (EU) is taken into account, the crime rates are even more astounding.

Additionally, there are studies that reveal when gun control laws are relaxed, crime rates actually go down. As Thomas Jefferson wrote in his "Commonplace Book" in the 1774-1776 timeframe, "Laws that forbid the carrying of arms . . . disarm only those who are neither inclined nor determined to commit crimes . . . Such laws make things worse for the assaulted and better for the assailants; they serve rather to encourage than to prevent homicides, for an unarmed man may be attacked with greater confidence than an armed man." One of our fore fathers articulated it much better than I could ever hope. Therefore, remain vigilant of your rights and be proactive in ensuring they are maintained.

As you can tell, I am an ardent opponent of gun control laws that prevent the law abiding citizen from owning self defense firearms. However, I am a strong believer in stiff penalties for criminals who use firearms to carryout their crimes.

That is enough of my soapbox stand on individual rights to the ownership of firearms and punishment of criminals.

Forty-eight states and the District of Columbia all have some form of concealed weapons carry permitting system. However, the District of Columbia does not define what theirs is, so for all intent and purpose they are not a weapon carry issue governmental entity. Two states have denied their citizens' right to concealed carry – Illinois and Wisconsin.

All of these states can be placed into one of five categories – shall issue to residents only, shall issue to residents and non-residents, may issue to residents only, may issue to residents and non-residents, and right denied.

Shall Issue to Residents Only:

There are 21 states with shall issue laws. Shall issue means that upon application and after meeting minimum requirements set by the state legislature, a resident must be issued a concealed carry permit in the following states:

- Alaska
- Arkansas
- Colorado
- Georgia
- Kansas
- Kentucky
- Louisiana
- Michigan
- Mississippi
- Missouri
- Montana
- Nebraska
- New Mexico
- North Carolina

- Ohio
- Oklahoma
- South Dakota
- Tennessee

- Vermont
- West Virginia
- Wyoming

Shall Issue to Residents and Non-Residents:

Seventeen states have shall issue laws that apply to both residents and non-residents. Again, shall issue means that after meeting requirements set forth by the state legislature, both residents and non-residents shall be issued a concealed carry permit. The following states fall within this category:

- Arizona
- Florida
- Idaho
- Indiana
- Maine
- Minnesota
- Nevada
- New Hampshire
- North Dakota

- Oregon
- Pennsylvania
- Rhode Island
- South Carolina
- Texas
- Utah
- Virginia
- Washington

May Issue to Residents Only:

May issue differs from shall issue laws. In a may issue jurisdiction citizens do not necessarily have a right to carry a handgun, but may be allowed to do so under certain circumstances. There are six such states in this category, which are listed below:

- Alabama
- California
- Delaware

- Hawaii
- New York
- District of Columbia

May Issue to Residents and Non-Residents:

Five states have may issue laws that apply to both residents and non-residents. They are similar to the previous category except they apply to non-residents as well. These five states are:

- Connecticut
- Iowa
- Maryland
- Massachusetts
- New Jersey

Right Denied:

Unfortunately, there are two states that outright deny their citizens the right of carrying a firearm in a concealed manner. These two states are Illinois and Wisconsin. In Illinois it is unlawful to actually own or possess a firearm of any kind without first obtaining a Firearms Owner's Identification Card, also known as a FOID. Without a FOID one cannot even have a weapon in their own home. The FOID does not grant permission to carry a weapon, only to own or possess the weapon – so much for constitutional rights in Illinois. It is the Illinois State Police who issue the FOID.

Wisconsin is not as draconian as Illinois in their gun laws. However, they do not issue concealed carry permits. There is no law preventing open carry of firearms, but this is not a common occurrence there, and would most likely be discouraged.

Reciprocity

Many states recognize concealed carry permits issued by other states. These reciprocity laws change periodically, so when carrying a weapon one should check the state in which they intend to travel for specifics about that state's reciprocity. Also, each state's weapon transport laws differ as to where the weapon must be, whether it must be unloaded, and whether it should be in plain view or can be concealed in the glove box or console. Again, check before transporting a weapon across state lines.

An excellent internet web site for checking on reciprocity is USA Carry, which can be found at the following URL:

http://www.usacarry.com/concealed_carry_permit_informatio n.html

Another excellent web site for checking concealed carry laws is the National Rifle Association – Institute for Legislative Action, whose URL is:

http://www.nraila.org/gunlaws/

Flying Armed

Private Citizens cannot actually fly armed – that is having the weapon on them while in the passenger compartment. Nor can private citizens have firearms in any carryon bags. Law enforcement officers can be armed or have a firearm in the passenger cabin of a commercial aircraft under certain conditions and after completing the proper paperwork.

Private Citizens can carry their defensive handguns or long guns with them to their destination on commercial aircraft in their checked baggage. Weapons must be declared to the airline at check in and be contained in a hard side lockable case within the locked suitcase. Following are the rules stipulated by the Department of Homeland Security, Transportation Security Administration (DHS/TSA): The key regulatory requirements to transporting firearms, firearm parts or ammunition in checked baggage are:

- You must declare all firearms to the airline during the ticket counter check-in process.
- The firearm must be unloaded.
- The firearm must be in a hard-sided container.
- The container must be locked. A locked container is defined as one that completely secures the firearm from access by anyone other than you. Cases that can be pulled open with little effort do not meet this criterion.
- TSA recommends that you provide the key or combination to the security officer if they need to open the container. You should remain present during screening to take the key back after the container is cleared. If you are not present and the security officer must open the container, TSA or the airline will make a reasonable attempt to contact you. If you cannot be contacted, the container will not be placed on the plane. Federal regulations prohibit unlocked gun cases (or cases with broken locks) on aircraft.
- You must securely pack any ammunition in fiber (such as cardboard), wood or metal boxes or other packaging that is specifically designed to carry small amounts of ammunition.
- You can't use firearm magazines for packing ammunition unless they completely and securely enclose the ammunition (e.g., by securely covering the exposed portions of the magazine or by securely placing the magazine in a pouch, holder, holster or lanyard).
- You may carry the ammunition in the same hard-sided case as the firearm, as long as you pack it as described above.
- You can't bring black powder or percussion caps used with black-powder type firearms in either your carry-on or checked baggage.

TSA and other authorities strictly enforce these regulations. Violations can result in criminal prosecution and civil penalties of up to $10,000 per violation.

Airlines have their own additional requirements on the carriage of firearms and the amount of ammunition that you may have in your checked baggage. Therefore, travelers should also contact the airline regarding its firearm and ammunition carriage policies. Most airlines have these requirements posted on their web sites. Know these requirements before going to the airport, so you do not wind up having to leave your weapon at home because it does not meet the airline's requirements.

Chapter 11

Additional Resources

The Constitution of most of our states (and of the United States) assert that all power is inherent in the people; that they may exercise it by themselves; that it is their right and duty to be at all times armed and that they are entitled to freedom of person, freedom of religion, freedom of property, and freedom of press.

Thomas Jefferson

Throughout the book I have mentioned a number of organizations devoted to the preservation of the shooting sports. Each of the following sections briefly describes the purpose of each organization and how one can further explore their mission and offerings. Enjoy!

National Rifle Association (NRA)

Since 1871, the NRA has promoted firearms and hunting activities. It also is the most organized defender of the individual's Second Amendment Right to own firearms. There are many programs sponsored by the NRA such as hunter and firearms safety, marksmanship training, and general public firearms education programs. Additionally, it has an arm devoted to tracking and influencing gun legislation at the local, state, and federal levels. If your individual right of gun ownership is important, this is the organization to join. Its web site is located at:

http://www.nra.org/home.aspx

USA Carry

USA Carry began in March 2007, when its developer set up a website for Nevadans focused on Nevada concealed carry information. When the author of the website was about to move to Florida, he thought a similar website for Florida was a good idea. In conducting research for a Florida website, the author determined that what was the largest concealed carry website had been permanently taken off the web, so USA Carry was born.

This website now provides concealed carry information for every state of the United States. An easy to use reciprocity map is available for determining where your state's permit is accepted. There are more than 5,000 members active in a number of online forums, blogs, groups, etc. It is truly a useful resource that can be found at:

http://www.usacarry.com/

United States Practical Shooting Association (USPSA)

USPSA is the American region of the International Practical Shooting Confederation (IPSC). IPSC began in California during the late 1950s. It was established to promote, maintain, and advance practical marksmanship. USPSA's mission is to promote safe, fair and fun participation in practical shooting competition. Its members consist of all ages and skill levels. USPSA local competitions are a fun way of improving and maintaining your defensive handgun skills. More information can be obtained by accessing their web site at:

http://www.uspsa.org/

International Defensive Pistol Association (IDPA)

IDPA, founded in 1996, is devoted to a shooting sport

that simulates self-defense scenarios and real life encounters. Founders of IDPA developed the sport around self-defense and not competition. No special equipment is needed. Practical guns and gear are required. Its main goal is to test the skill of the individual, not equipment or gamesmanship. Again, local IDPA matches can help improve and maintain your defensive handgun skills. To find out more, visit their web site at:

http://www.idpa.com/

There are many more web sites that exist devoted to the defensive handgunner. Search the internet for the term "defensive handgun" and more than 300,000 web pages are listed. Many of these can help you further explore defensive hand gunning.

Epilogue

*A good plan, violently executed now, is better than a
perfect plan next week.*
General George S. Patton, Jr.

Do not stop your quest for becoming a better defensive
handgunner with this book. Continue to learn and practice
the techniques presented in this book. Add tools to your
individual tool box so that when faced with a deadly force
situation you respond accurately, powerfully, and speedily.

It has been a pleasure writing this book. Thank you for
reading. I hope you are never faced with having to use
deadly force for your self protection or the protection of a
loved one, but if ever you do, I hope the information on these
pages help you in some small way to survive the encounter!

I will leave you with an ending that one of my colleagues
used to give when sending off our most recent graduates:

Stay Alert

Stay In Shape

And Stay Alive!"

INDEX